"In this new resource for preaching, Kent Anderson speaks to those of us who want to give the best of Holy Scripture—and of movemental change now—to our congregations. We are reminded that our learning outcome is formation and true discipleship—preaching is one important means and not the end. Let us all pray for the impact of this powerful new book!"

—**Graham Singh**, executive director, Church Planting Canada; rector, St. Jax Montreal

"Integration brings wholeness to fragmented parts. That's what Kent Anderson's new book does for preaching. Most importantly, he connects preaching to God's great purposes: *"God is at work. There is a trajectory to history. The world and all that is within is moving toward God's eternal purpose. That purpose has culminated in the cross. When we preach, we embrace that purpose. Our proclamation places us within the flow of movement God has propelled."* If that were the only uplifting and renewing truth, it would make this book worthwhile. But he thoughtfully connects each of the multiple parts of sermon preparation and delivery to this ultimate goal. The result is a hope-filled and energizing tutorial for all who seek to refresh and renew their calling to preach more effectively."

—**Leland Eliason**, executive director and provost emeritus, Bethel Seminary

INTEGRATIVE PREACHING

A COMPREHENSIVE MODEL
for Transformational Proclamation

KENTON C. ANDERSON

Baker Academic

a division of Baker Publishing Group
Grand Rapids, Michigan

Published by Baker Academic
a division of Baker Publishing Group
PO Box 6287, Grand Rapids, MI 49516-6287
www.bakeracademic.com

Printed in the United States of America

Library of Congress Cataloging-in-Publication Data
Names: Anderson, Kenton C., author.
Title: Integrative preaching : a comprehensive model for transformational proclamation /
    Kenton C. Anderson.
Description: Grand Rapids : Baker Academic, 2017. | Includes bibliographical references and index.
Identifiers: LCCN 2017019663 | ISBN 9780801098871 (pbk. : alk. paper)
Subjects: LCSH: Preaching.
Classification: LCC BV4211.3 .A5355 2017 | DDC 251—dc23
LC record available at https://lccn.loc.gov/2017019663

17   18   19   20   21   22   23   7   6   5   4   3   2   1

In keeping with biblical principles of creation stewardship, Baker Publishing Group advocates the responsible use of our natural resources. As a member of the Green Press Initiative, our company uses recycled paper when possible. The text paper of this book is composed in part of post-consumer waste.

CONTENTS

Preface   vii

Introduction   ix

Part 1 Understanding the Integrative Model of Preaching

1. Preaching Is Integral (Cohesive)   3

2. Preaching Is Horizontal (Physical)   11

3. Preaching Is Vertical (Spiritual)   22

4. Preaching Is Centripetal (Kinetic)   33

Part 2 The Functional Elements of Integrative Preaching

5. The Story That Engages   45

6. The Theme That Instructs   56

7. The Gospel That Convicts   66

8. The Mission That Inspires   76

Part 3 The Material Compounds of Integrative Preaching

9. Problems: The Preacher as a Pastor   87

10. Points: The Preacher as a Theologian   94

11. Prayers: The Preacher as a Worshiper   102

12. Pictures: The Preacher as a Prophet   110

Part 4 The Method of Integrative Preaching

13. Discover the Message   121

14. Assemble the Sermon   132

15. Master the Outcome   145

16. Deliver the Event   155

Conclusion   165

Appendix: Sermon Examples   169

Suggested Reading   179

Postscript   183

Index   185

PREFACE

I have been teaching and writing about preaching for about twenty-five years. I have preached in hundreds of churches and conference centers to many thousands of people. After a while it starts to feel like experience, and experience always ought to be shared. This is not my first book on the subject of preaching, but it is my most comprehensive. It is not the only word on the subject, but it is a good word, and it is the best that I have to offer. If you work with these suggestions, I am confident you will be a more effective preacher, and that will be good for the kingdom, good for the church, and good for all of us who listen.

I am grateful to my students and readers across these years who have respected the process and given it a go. I appreciate the helpful comments and the opportunity to test these ideas across the canvas of a few thousand student sermons. I believe preaching is transformative, even when it is offered by students who are learning the craft. My faith has been nurtured by these opportunities to hear from God.

I am grateful to my colleagues, who have trusted me with the students we have mutually loved.

I am grateful to my listeners, who have sat under the sound of my preaching. I trust that you have heard from God and have been transformed by what our God has said to you.

I am particularly grateful to my family, who continue to encourage me and who value what I do. Those who know my wife, Karen, will recognize her input on many of these pages. In her chaplaincy work with senior citizens, she has had many opportunities to test these thoughts in action.

I am most especially grateful to God, who has been pleased to make himself known in the world through the preaching of his Word. I am amazed and gratified that he has been willing to use me in this work that is so central to his heart.

> Additional materials helpful in learning
> and sharing the principles in this book
> can be found at www.preaching.org.

INTRODUCTION

Preaching is a particularly confident way of speaking. When a football coach says that he is "preaching defense" to his team, he is speaking in an especially authoritative mode, welcome on the practice field, though less so elsewhere. A player's job depends on the pleasure of his coach. His is not to question why. His is to defend or die. The player must presume the coach's authority if he wants to keep his job. Coaches can preach. Others might better hold their tongue.

The places where we welcome preaching are few and seldom. A parent, perhaps, could preach to a child until a certain age. A deeply trusted friend could adopt the role of preacher, though perhaps in sparing measure. A pastor preaches as the function of his or her calling, which is a complicated matter.

There was a time when preaching was in vogue—when people were willing to grant authority to the man of the cloth who spoke for God among the people. There was a time when people were comfortable submitting to authority. That time is not today. No one is going to grant you privilege because you are a preacher. No social or financial benefit is going to come your way. You may have to pay relational capital instead of gaining it. To read this book and put its principles into practice might require of you a kind of courage. The day when preaching brought a sense of cultural privilege is long past.

In fact, many will see preaching as unwelcome, and sometimes even rude. Polite society agrees that we must not speak of things that demand or divide. Preaching is just too confident—arrogant even. Our subject too threatening. Our conclusions too demanding. Friends don't let friends attend to sermons.

And yet here we are, you and I, sharing thoughts around this theme of preaching. The Bible is clear, and our calling is unshaken. We must preach the Word, despite the constant opposition we will have to deal with. We remember that Paul told Timothy to expect a time when people would not put up with what we have to say—that they would turn their heads instead to those whose words would soothe the itching of their ears. We understand that this is the way of things, and we would not expect it to be any different.

There are those who have an ear for this. We understand that preachers travel narrow roads, but we understand that those pathways lead to special places. We believe we preach in the presence of God and of Christ Jesus and that we will be accountable for what we have to say. If we can keep our head and do the work of our callings, we will find that there are those God has especially prepared to respond to what we have to say—to what *he* has to say.

And so we preach, when it seems to be in season and when it seems to be out of season, when we find it convenient and when we find it inconvenient, when we are fairly sure they want to hear what we have to say and when we are quite sure they don't. We preach because we have been called to it—because we could do no other. We preach for those who will find Jesus, and we preach the accountability of those who won't. We preach because someone has to, because there is a harvest to be reaped, and because we just love to speak of Jesus.

We Preach Because God Speaks

Is there anything better than that God has spoken? And not just that he has spoken, but also that he speaks? Set aside any doubts or postmodern uncertainties, if only for the moment. Imagine that the God of the universe, who spoke the world into being, is not disinterested in his creation. Imagine that this God is invested in the outcome. Consider the idea that this God is actively engaged, sustaining things and speaking things. Imagine that the God who built you from dirt has a purpose for you forever and that he has something to say to you. Would you not want to listen?

God spoke in his initiation of creation, establishing the world and its direction by the power of his Word. He spoke in the incarnation of Christ, who showed God to us, offering his mind and ultimately setting the terms and paving the way for our salvation. He spoke through his inspired Word, the record of his will and of his way. And now he speaks through the convergence of these means and by the illumination of his Spirit. Whenever we stand to preach, we bring this all together. As we speak in the presence of God, of the person of Christ, through the purpose of Scripture, in the power of the Spirit, the kingdom comes and is populated by those prepared to hear—if we are prepared to preach.

We do not do this out of hubris, as if the power were of our own contrivance. None of us is good enough or wise enough or eloquent enough to achieve these outcomes by the power of our words. We are not that powerful—not that influential. We are not wealthy enough, or attractive enough, or anything enough to achieve the purposes of God for our preaching.

Some of us know this too truly—our not-enough-ness. It is dispiriting to give yourself to something when you know that you will never be enough. Our vision for our preaching can fade. Our confidence in the effectiveness of our preaching can settle into a weekly incrementalism that you have to trust by faith because it is hard to see the fruit on any given Sunday. This can happen when we forget what God is doing and who it is who speaks.

God Is the Preacher of His Word

We have come to something key—something that will render everything else this book offers as useless if we cannot apprehend it. Let me put it as a question: Who is the preacher, anyway?

"Well, I am," we stammer uncertainly, sensing a trick to the question. "I am the one standing here in front of the crowd. I am the one they're going to talk about if I fail to feed them in the manner to which they are accustomed. I am the vulnerable one. I am the one responsible."

And about that you are correct. But I would press the question further. Who is it who speaks, and who is it who listens? Who has the words of everlasting life? Whose words have the power to transform?

Not yours. Certainly not mine. It is not the words of the human preacher that will bring the kingdom. I have words, and some of them are worth speaking. I do have opinions, and some of them are worth hearing. You could do worse. But nobody ought to come to hear me preach. We ought to come to hear the voice of God.

God is the preacher. It is the self-revealing God who brings us words of truth and life. It is God to whom we ought to give attention. It is he who offers hope and healing. God preaches, and that is both wonder and comfort to the beleaguered human who has felt the weekly burden as if it was his or her own.

It is this theological foundation that gives hope to our preaching. The doctrine of revelation—this appreciation that the Creator spoke and speaks—is the thing that animates our preaching. As humans we can see ourselves as conduits or culverts—channeling the flow of God's communication.

We Are Listeners to the Sermon That God Preaches

And yet we are something more than that. This metaphor of culverts, giant concrete channels, is uninspiring—belittling even to the privilege that is ours as human preachers. We are more than channels, more than heralds, more than ambassadors, more than facilitators of God's message, though we are all that, yet more. We are listeners—first listeners—and there is glory in it.

God does not speak into a void. This is a communication process that requires both sender and receiver. Without reception there is no preaching. Without a listener, preaching is an incomplete pass. The tree that falls in the forest makes no sound until there is an ear to hear it. The glory of preaching is not only in the speaking of it, but in the hearing also. The hearing is the human part.

There is great dignity in this. That God speaks and we can hear him bestows a special privilege. Craig Brian Larson has said that in preaching "gravity reverses," and that nothing offers greater dignity than the preaching and the hearing of a sermon.[1]

Human preachers have a special place within this process. Preachers are less communicators than they are listeners—special listeners, first listeners, with the advantage of a head start. We get there first, ahead of the crowd, and know the joy of first discovery. We engage the text, seeking the Spirit, and we hear! We hear the voice of God, who speaks to us his grace and truth. Then having heard, we take what we have heard and offer it to others. God comes with us as we do. God keeps speaking by his Word and by his Spirit, in a trinitarian expression of his intention for the world and life and us. We speak, certainly in that we give voice to language, but it is not our language. It is his Word that we heard first and now help others, that they might also hear.

Preaching as an Act of Leadership

Preaching is an act of leadership, like the time I led a group of guys to the top of Black Tusk. I had been to the mountain before, and I had seen the

---

1. "But then they hear anointed preaching, and gravity reverses as people sense the upward pull of heaven." Craig Brian Larson, "A Weekly Dose of Condensed Dignity," in *The Art and Craft of Biblical Preaching: A Comprehensive Resource for Today's Communicators*, ed. Haddon Robinson and Craig Brian Larson (Grand Rapids: Zondervan, 2005), 30.

beauty of its vistas. I loved these young men, and I wanted for them to know the same exhilaration that I had first felt when I scaled the summit. So I took them there and gave them the advantage of my experience. Because I had seen, I could help them to see. Some of them, no doubt, would grow to see even further than I, which is a tremendous thing.

Hearing is also an awesome thing. The human preacher hears and then leads others to hear. We lead in listening, which is the best, certainly the most condensed expression of human preaching that I know. Preaching is *leading in listening*—listening to the voice of God and helping others do the same. The assumption is that when we have done so, things change—seen and unseen. Nothing can remain the same when we have heard from God. Believe that with all the faith you have.

When we preach, then, we express a wonderful oxymoron that I first heard from Leonard Sweet: humbled confidence.[2] We are humbled because the Word is not our own. We are confident because the Word is his.

These are not just empty words, as if words ever lack substance. Speech matters. It is not for nothing that God spoke the world into being. It is not accidental that the Son of God is described as "living Word." Words have implications, and the Word of God carries consequence forever. When we get this, we will open our mouths and speak with the humbled confidence that leads others to listen to the words that change the world. This is what it is to preach.

Preaching Happens Many Places

We might take a moment to discuss who and where. There are those among us who are preachers in a professional sense, by which I mean only that it is a function of their employment for which they may even be offered pay. This is not to be despised. Scripture describes this as a noble calling with special accountability, to which honor and respect are due. But there are others who will also preach.

Whenever we lead in listening to the Word, whoever leads and wherever it happens, we find preaching, and it always is in season. Let us not disrespect the preaching that happens in coffee shops and homes on Wednesday nights and Saturday mornings, by women and men of all types and callings. Let us celebrate whenever someone intends to help someone else hear through

---

2. "A right spirit from a biblical standpoint is the oxymoronic combination of confidence and humility." Leonard Sweet, *SoulTsunami: Sink or Swim in New Millennium Culture* (Grand Rapids: Zondervan, 1999), 312.

persuasive, intentional communication of the Word of God. It might be out-lined on a napkin, or diagrammed on YouTube. It may be shared over tea, or from a wooden pulpit. Wherever it happens, God is there, and he is speaking, and so we celebrate.

Of course, it can always be done better. The human element in this process can be done well or poorly. Well done is always better, and to that we must aspire. That it is God who speaks does not relieve us of the need to bring our best. In fact, it is the opposite. That it is God who speaks inspires us to bring our best.

This book is about bringing our best. I have been doing this for a long time, both preaching and teaching others to preach. I have learned some things along the way that seem to have been helpful. As I share with you, I trust that you will be led to a more effective way of leading others. This will be honoring to the Lord, and it will be good for people. So I will bring my best, and I trust you will bring your best effort likewise. Feel free to think critically and to challenge what you read. Take the stuff that strikes you as worthy and build it into your practice with as much faith as you can muster. But as you do, do not forget who does the preaching. Remember that it is not you.

The following chapters will take you all the way from a theological con-ception of integrative preaching to the production and delivery of sermons that follow this model. The first section of the book will be theoretical. The final section will be applied. In between we will sketch out the functions and materials that put our model into practice.

This model might differ from those you have learned elsewhere. But if you look closely, you might recognize your former learnings in the larger frame-work. I am offering an integrative model that naturally seeks to subsume and incorporate various legitimate ways of being within preaching. However, you might need to prepare yourself to be taken further than where you might otherwise have found yourself. Preaching has a lot more to offer than what many of us have so far realized.

I will soon have a lot to say about integration, of course, but let me jump ahead by offering one of the most profound integrative aspects to the prac-tice of our preaching—the integration of Spirit and servant.[3] Practicing the

---

3. This book is the development in full of the final chapter of my last book, which sketched the landscape of preaching at the time. In that book I described four fundamental models: declarative, pragmatic, narrative, and visionary preaching. The final chapter was dedicated to this integrative possibility: integrative preaching. See Kenton C. Anderson, *Choosing to Preach: A Comprehensive Introduction to Sermon Options and Structures* (Grand Rapids: Zondervan, 2006).

principles you will read within these pages must always be an act of service. No matter how good you get at these things, you will never make unnecessary the work of God's Holy Spirit. This is the great mystery inherent in our preaching—that the Spirit would unite with the servant, such that the Word of God is heard. This is our joy whenever we lead in listening to God.

PART 1

Understanding the Integrative Model of Preaching

My wife and I purchased our current home prior to its construction. Talk about an act of faith. Committing hundreds of thousands of dollars on a home that doesn't exist yet might be an act of confidence, or it might be an act of ignorance. It was helpful to us that the developer offered us a model. This miniature physical replica of the building allowed us to imagine the possibility of living there. When we eventually moved into our condominium, we were amazed to see how accurately the model projected the actual.

This book presents a model for integrative preaching. It will be helpful for preachers to gain a conceptual overview of the task. The better we can understand the model, the more likely we are to be able to replicate the practice. The preaching that happens in the context of community most often happens on a schedule. Week by week the preacher prepares and presents the message

1

intended from the Word. If we are going to be able to sustain an ongoing intentional and purposeful plan for preaching, it will help us to work from a reliable model.

The integrative model of preaching lays across two axes, the horizontal and the vertical, in a kind of map of the homiletic landscape. The horizontal (physical) axis overlays the vertical (spiritual) axis in the shape of the cross. As the sermon moves, it works by centripetal force to draw everything toward the center point. Head integrates with heart, and heaven comes in contact with the human. The model leads us to a set of elements and compounds that become helpful in our work of preaching.

The next four chapters will sketch out theory behind the integrative preaching model. We will think biblically and theologically. We will dig into texts in Scripture. In so doing, we will lay the groundwork for the practical instruction that is to come. We will preach well when we understand our task and grasp the nature of this integration.

This conceptual model of preaching describes the manner in which transformational force can be applied. It all comes together in an act of listening, as the self-revealing God achieves his purpose. More than just a model, the cross becomes the means by which we are made congruent with our Creator. Having heard from God, we are transformed by the message. We become integrated in the Spirit to the purpose of the cross.

1

Preaching Is Integral (Cohesive)

Living well is about finding integration. It is about cohesion—overcoming the disintegration of elements that pull apart and separate. We often feel the need to choose between things like head and heart, heaven and human, with the result that we *dis*integrate. We fall to pieces, unproductive and unfulfilled.

Integration offers the idea that separated elements can be united in a single substance such that the integrity of each element might be sustained. Integration is about finding wholeness, as can be seen by its cognate expressions. An integer is a whole number, not a fractional number. Something that is "integral" is something that is necessary or essential to the wholeness or completion of a larger entity. A bridge requires "structural integrity" if we are to trust it with our weight. Integration, then, is about the cohesion of elements such that the integrity of each remains undiminished and without compromise.

This kind of integration is necessary if life is going to work. A baseball pitcher's effectiveness depends on the ability to integrate power and control. A relationship's durability depends on the ability of two people to be able to form a union out of unique human characteristics, without diminishing the integrity of either individual.

I have been married a long time. I would say that my marriage to Karen has effectively modeled the biblical ideal of two becoming one. Our lives have been integrated in every possible way—physically, financially, socially, and spiritually. We are, somehow, indissoluble. And yet we are still ourselves. Karen's personality is intact. She is still the woman I first met so many years ago. I believe that I am still the same person also. I may be older and heavier, but I am still me. Marriage does not diminish the personhood or personality

3

of the individual partner. It simply makes something more of the individual partners to the mutual benefit of both. You could say that my wife and I are integrated.

The Integrative Nature of the Bible

If you don't understand integration, you will not really understand the Bible. Integration is seen throughout the Scriptures. Marriage is just one of many biblical expressions of this reality. The church, for example, has struggled for centuries to appreciate how God's sovereignty relates to human responsibility. How can women and men live with the freedom of their choices if God is sovereignly determining the course of the universe? How is it possible that Jesus can exist as both God and man, his two natures coexisting without compromise? What does it mean that the Word became flesh? Words are intangible, conceptual expressions, but flesh is meaty and grounded. That this Word could express the fundamental truths of the universe, transcending all of creation while consisting of the very stuff of creation—earth and dust and blood and guts—requires the most profound integrity.

"The Word became flesh and made his dwelling among us. We have seen his glory, the glory of the one and only Son . . . full of grace and truth" (John 1:14). This is a profound theological oxymoron that must be integrated if it is going to carry the intention of the text. Truth can weigh heavy when dealt with a hard and determinative hand. Grace can seem light and untethered from the considerations and consequences that truth requires. But if the two can find a sense of integration, we can appreciate the integrity that Jesus bore and which seems to lie within the heart of God.

Integrative Option 1: The Coin

One model worth considering is the *coin*. A coin has two sides, each equal to the other—heads and tails. You cannot entertain the one without a spurning of the other. Have you ever tried to view both sides of a coin at the same time? Go ahead and give it a try. Take a coin out of your pocket and see whether you can do it. The only thing you can do with a coin is to flip it—heads or tails, one or the other. You cannot have both sides. You must make your choice.

The coin is effective as a means of gaining clarity. One can step around the muddle by simply committing to one's choice. The coin is activated by the word *or*. It offers divinity *or* humanity, Word *or* flesh, grace *or* truth. But while such a choice offers the benefit of focus, it comes at an unacceptable price.

the coin

heads   tails

"or"

Integrative Option 2: The Continuum

A second model is the *continuum*. On a continuum, *dis*integrated elements are established in polar opposition. One then locates oneself somewhere along the continuum in between the separated options. This model requires compromise. Moving in the direction of one alternative comes at the expense of the other.

The advantage of this model is that it offers fluidity. One can move back and forth along the continuum without a fixed sense of finality. The continuum is identified by the conjunction *yet*. Jesus was human, *yet* he was also God. Christ is the Word, *yet* he is also flesh. He offers grace, *yet* he offers truth as well. There is a sense of regret about the matter, that the one is compromised by the presence of the other. Word is moderated by flesh. Grace is countered by truth. The emphasis of one requires some abandonment of the other, though perhaps just temporarily.

the continuum

Peter ▬▬▬▬▬▬▬▬▬▬▬▬▬ Paul

"yet"

The normal way to function on a continuum is to try to find the center point, equidistant from the severed poles. It is an attempt to find a kind of balance, whereby each element finds an evened weight. But these attempts at balance are usually inadequate, given that they almost always require unwelcome compromise. The typical way of balance is to take from one side in order to give to the other—we rob Peter to pay Paul, and in so doing, both become less than what we would otherwise hope for.

Balance can leave a person wanting. You can have two flat tires in balance with one another, but they are not going to get you very far. What we really need is a model that will not require a sense of compromise. We need to go one hundred miles an hour down both roads at the same time.

Integrative Option 3: The Cross

The most promising model is the *cross*. The cross is an integrative model wherein the horizontal overlays the vertical, creating intersection. The cross is a way of picturing cohesion instead of choice or compromise. Mathematically it describes a plus sign, indicating the addition of one element to the other.

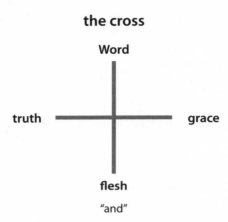

the cross

The cross aspires to a new and heightened form of unity, expecting something greater, beyond the possibility offered by less holistic options. The cross is driven by the genius of *and*.[1] We observe this theologically in the actual cross on which Jesus died and all that it represents. Jesus himself is humanity *and* divinity, Word *and* flesh. His death on the cross spoke of grace *and* truth. As we think toward our model of preaching, we can similarly see the possibilities available through integration, where the addition of one thing to another can lead to something greater than the sum of individual parts.

Just as plotting one's global position requires the fixing of both latitude and longitude, our formation in Christ requires both the horizontal and the vertical dimensions. Horizontally, we appreciate the physical nature of our life on earth. Human beings are grounded—subject to gravity as we live and move on the earth. We all appreciate that somehow we were made for more. We hold within ourselves a latent aspiration for something that might transcend what we can reach within our grasp. We long for heaven, but heaven is beyond us.

1. James C. Collins and Jerry I. Porras, "No 'Tyranny of the Or' (Embrace the 'Genius of the And')," in *Built to Last: Successful Habits of Visionary Companies* (New York: Harper-Business, 1994), 43–45.

Another way to put this is that we are more than merely material. As human beings, we are both physical and spiritual beings. We have been formed with the capacity to appreciate the transcendent. Having been created in the image of God, we are hardwired to know God and to recognize his voice. But our knowledge of God is dependent on his willingness to make the introduction. Living horizontally, we cannot command his presence or his power. We depend on his initiative to make himself known within the world.

Vertically, we understand our spiritual dependence on the God who was willing to come down from heaven to engage us at the point of our need in the context of the created earth. The vertical line moves from the top down in description of his incarnation. The downward movement of the cross describes God's loving condescension. He literally descended, eschewing the glories of heaven in exchange for the opportunity of our salvation here on earth. The vertical line is a symbol of God's willingness to pursue us on our terms—working our ground to overcome the problem of our sin.

The cross, then, is both the model and the means of our formation. Physically, the cross was the instrument on which the Lord Jesus Christ made the ultimate sacrifice for us. Theologically, the cross also models the integration of the material and the spiritual, heaven and earth, in the person of Jesus and for the good of all God's children.

The Benefits of Cross-Shaped Integration

The benefits of a cross-shaped integration are experienced on many levels. For example, an emphasis on the physical guards against the potential for an untethered spirituality, just as a concern for the spiritual serves as an antidote against the threat of a myopic materialism. This dual emphasis keeps both elements from careening into unhelpful and unhealthy extremes. But integration offers more than mere correction.

Integration empowers, even multiplies, the other. An emphasis on grace is only deepened by its corresponding truth. For example, people often offer forgiveness by belittling the hurt that they have felt.

"Will you forgive me?"

"Don't worry about it," comes the answer. "It's no big deal."

No big deal? Of course it is a big deal. Whenever someone sins against another, causing someone else pain, it is significant. Hurt is not forgiven by pretending that it does not exist. It may seem like the only way to repair or sustain relationship is by downgrading the actual impact of another person's action, but this is a cheap and irresilient way of bandaging pain.

Grace is most fully present when we deeply and profoundly experience our pain and see it for its ugliness, but then still find ourselves capable of offering forgiveness. This is grace magnified by an integrated awareness of the truth.

Another benefit is the way that integration overcomes inherent limitations. An exclusive attention to physical reality restricts one to those things that can be measured. A purely material universe disallows any consideration of more transcendent possibilities. Metaphysical approaches are ruled entirely out of hand. The strong survive in such robust environments. Spiritual sensitivities seem superfluous in a world that survives solely on its strength.

Most of us know better. Life is more than just material. We sense a greater, deeper truth that travels above and beyond the things we see and touch. Gravity is intolerable as a force that keeps us grounded. Physical reality seems common and prosaic once one has touched the skies. And yet to locate one's truth entirely in the spiritual is to make oneself irrelevant to the lives we live on earth. To be heavenly minded, we are told, can make us of no earthly or tangible good.

This is why we integrate. Appreciating the spiritual does not eliminate our interest in the physical, but it mitigates the weakness of a mere materialism. Finding value in the material does not have to compete with the spiritual as if there were not the space for both. A spiritual interest, rather, keeps material reality from contracting into meaninglessness. A physical interest ensures that the spiritual does not fritter into foolishness. The one completes the other by fulfilling the promise represented by each.

Change is spoken into being. How we talk to one another and to ourselves will be formative of both our lives and our souls. If our speech is narrow and disintegrated, we will produce narrow and disintegrated lives. If our speech embodies a cohesive integration, it will resonate with vivid color.

Speech matters. Formation happens as we talk truth to one another. Our sermons and soliloquies, our conversations and consultations all have power to shape and form the habits of our hearts. Whether we are talking to ourselves or talking to each other, we need to talk well. We need to offer the kind of talk that is modeled in the cross.

Usually we call this "preaching." Others might call it discipleship or spiritual formation. Some may just think of it as being an encourager, making the most of an opportunity to offer needed blessing through speaking, nudging, challenging, or maybe even blogging, tweeting, or some other means of social interaction. However we describe our opportunity, we would best see our task as integrative, laying horizontal over vertical in the manner of the cross.

Horizontal and Vertical: Physical and Spiritual

The horizontal line of the cross designates the *physical* axis, describing life as we know it as it unfolds in real life. Think of the horizontal line as signifying the ground on which we walk and form our lives. Think of this line representing our life as it unfolds in time and the effect on us of gravity. We are held tightly to the earth and all that it implies of us. We are material beings who perceive all of life either by cognition or affection. We think things and we feel things, sometimes by tactile touch and other times by means of our emotions, and that is all we know of life on the earth. We know what we experience within time. This is life on the ground—the horizontal line.

horizontal

physical
axis

The vertical line of the cross designates the *spiritual* axis, describing the relationship of heaven to the human. The top-to-bottom visual offered by the vertical line depicts for us the promise of something more than just our groundedness. Spiritually, we are always looking up, not only around. We are compelled by the thought that there is something greater, something beyond the limits of our physical experience. While there are those who try to tell us that this is only an immature wishfulness, we could counter as to why this wish occurs at all—where it comes from and why it is ubiquitous. Common to all humanity is this cosmic metaphysic, this sense that we are more than just the molecules that make up our material existence. This is the life of the soul, and it touches human to heaven—the vertical line.

The integrative model overlays the two—the vertical lying over the horizontal, the spiritual over the physical—in the form of the cross. The cross, as we have said, is a plus sign. It describes not a choice between options but the addition of one to the other—head plus heart and heaven added to the human. This is the horizontal and the vertical finding unity in the cross and

vertical

spiritual
axis

in the person of the cross—the Lord Jesus Christ. The cross, then, is not only the means of our salvation but the model also.

The movement of our preaching, then, creates a centripetal force, pulling all toward the center, the point where all things intersect and integrate. It is the cross that exerts this integrating force, drawing us in toward the heart of God, where otherwise we would be propelled out and to oblivion.

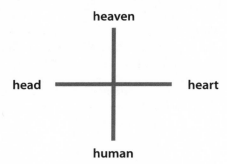

Integrative preaching is the manner and the substance of our speech. To speak of the cross is to talk about the gospel, the good and welcome message that God did not leave us to our ground, frustrated by the force of gravity, which keeps us incapable of rising to the heavens. This world is full of wonders, but there is a limit to what we know and what we can speak of here on earth. Cross talk tells us of the God who acted vertically, descending from on high to bring heaven to the human. For us as humans, earth is all that we have known, with heaven far beyond us. But God brought heaven down to earth in the shape of the cross and in the person of Jesus Christ.

Jesus lived and talked the cross and its purposes before he ever got to Calvary. John, one of his best friends and closest disciples, wrote that Jesus came as the Word become flesh and that his message, life, and manner spoke of grace and truth (John 1:14). This is the essence of integration—the cross, embodied and expressed. To this we must give voice.

2

Preaching Is Horizontal (Physical)

One of the most compelling motion pictures of 2013 was *Gravity*, Alfonso Cuarón's gripping depiction of the human endeavor to exist in space. Despite the science-fiction genre, the movie offered no monsters or intergalactic terrorists. The villain in the movie was outer space itself. Unleashed from the constraints of gravity, the characters played by Sandra Bullock and George Clooney cannot sustain their lives. Life, it seems, depends on gravity—a rootedness to the earth that sustains us and helps us find our footings.

If integration is about overcoming the disintegration that pulls apart and separates, gravity is the force that pulls things together and creates reality of substance. Gravity is the force that causes any two objects in the universe to be drawn together. It is the reason that planets sustain their orbits and that we keep our place on earth.

Let go of a book, and it will fall to the ground. Jump into the air, and you will soon find yourself returned to earth. Gravity keeps us grounded. Without gravity we would float into infinity, like Clooney's character at the end of the movie. Untethered from the forces that keep him connected to the earth, life is no longer sustainable. He simply floats, propelled ever outward to his eternal demise—the ultimate centrifugal object.

Cuarón's movie ends with the striking image of Sandra Bullock's character returned to earth. Subject again to gravity, she crawls out of the mud—an image of the first creation. She is human, and she is grounded, literally, so that the earth itself clings to her very body.

The Physical Axis

We were created for life on earth. Subject to gravity, we find our substance and our meaning. This is the horizontal line of the cross, the physical axis, representing the material nature of life as we think and feel our way across time.

There has been an impulse in the church to discount our physical nature. We have been so tuned to the spiritual dimension that we have come to believe that our bodies are a kind of enemy to be dismissed and defeated. Many of us seem to have decided that the spiritual is good and that the material is bad. In a move that probably owes more to Plato than to the Bible, we have adopted an unwitting gnosticism that suspects that everything physical is to be discounted in favor of the spirituality that we esteem.

We see this in the premedieval figure Simeon Stylites, who determined to live his life on top of a pole so as to overcome the impulses of the flesh. Initially he built a pole six feet in height with a small platform on the top to support his unfortunate body. Eventually, embarrassed by the lack of risk represented by the pole's limited height, he built a second pole, this time sixty feet in height. He lived atop this pole for thirty years. His disciples brought him food, which was raised to him by a rope-and-pulley basket system. His waste was removed in the same manner.

Simeon's purpose was to mortify the body—to put to death the desires of his flesh. Dallas Willard, in *The Spirit of the Disciplines*, provides a long list of these who thought they honored God by this sort of repudiation of the bodies—people who lived in fly-infested swamps, others who refused to stand up or to sit down for years at a time.[1] These were people who abused and flagellated themselves in the misguided attempt to prove themselves worthy of the love of God.

Of course, the flesh *is* to be resisted. The Bible uses the word *flesh* to describe the base and evil impulses of our disintegrated souls. The body apart from the Spirit will fall apart. The desire of the eyes, the pride of life, the lust of the flesh combine to describe a life embroiled in self, turned in on itself without the necessary attachment to the Spirit (1 John 2:16).

But this is not to say that our physical nature is by design ungodly. God created us as physical beings, and what he has created is described as *good*— deeply and profoundly and eternally good. The promise of heaven is not that our bodies will be repudiated or destroyed but that God's physical creation will be re-created and perfected. What we do with our bodies matters to God, which is why bodily and sexual sin matters so greatly to him. We do not honor

1. Dallas Willard, *The Spirit of the Disciplines: Understanding How God Changes Lives* (New York: Harper & Row, 1988), 142–43.

God by escaping or exceeding our physical natures, but rather by utilizing our bodies in ways that are in keeping with his eternal purposes.

Our physical life as God created it is both thought about and felt. Integration on the horizontal level is about combining *head* and *heart*. It is both the determinations of the mind and the intentions of the will that make life rich and beautiful.

The Left Brain and the Right Brain

We sometimes speak of the left brain and the right brain. Left-brained people are considered to be more logical and rational, driven by data and analysis. Right-brained people, by contrast, are thought to be more interested in aesthetics and motivated by beauty, feeling, and a creative impulse. This has been a useful construct in helping us to understand people and the differences that we see in one another. We all know individuals who lean toward the logical or toward the creative. Seldom, however, do we see the two dichotomized as clearly as the theory might suggest.

Recent psychological studies have stepped back from the stark distinctions that the left/right construct seems to offer. Studies published by the American Psychological Association show, for example, that mathematical performance is enhanced when both hemispheres of the brain are working in collaboration.[2] While the lateral halves of the brain do express distinct capacities, one half cannot function effectively without the corresponding effect of the other. The rational part of the brain requires its more intuitive counterpart. The head must have the heart. Integration exists at the level of primary brain chemistry.

This is an important point for those of us who are trying to understand how we will persuade people by our preaching. We who have believed that our sole responsibility is to explain the logic of our messages might wonder why our preaching has had limited impact. Creative communicators might likewise wonder why a segment of their audience remains strangely unresponsive to their story-weaving. The answer is obvious to those who understand the way that our brain halves relate. It is never enough to simply describe the rational foundations of the truth.[3] Neither is it ever going to be sufficient to attempt

2. Michael O'Boyle, "The Brain's Left and Right Sides Seem to Work Together Better in Mathematically Gifted Middle-School Youth," American Psychological Association, April 11, 2004, http://www.apa.org/news/press/releases/2004/04/interhemispheric.aspx.

3. "At the core of interpersonal neurobiology is our proposal that mindsight permits us to direct the flow of energy and information toward integration. And integration . . . is seen to be at the heart of well-being." Daniel J. Siegel, *Mindsight: The New Science of Personal Transformation* (New York: Bantam, 2010), iBooks edition.

only to inspire. The best communication will always cross over from the left brain to the right and back again. Effective preachers and teachers will always span the entire horizontal spectrum.

Referring back to our integrative metaphors, it will not be sufficient to choose head over heart, or heart over head, as if we were flipping a coin. Nor will it be enough to lay the two across a continuum so that progress in the direction of the head comes at the expense of a concern for the heart (or vice versa). The only useful approach is to follow the model of the cross, overlaying head and heart and holding both together equally at exactly the same time.

Head and Heart

Having established our concern for integration of head and heart, it is worth further examining the difference between these two aspects of our physical being—our ability to think over against our capacity to feel. The first move toward integration of these elements is to overcome the prejudice that would lead us to discount the other.

horizontal

head	affective
cognitive	heart

Highly cognitive and propositional preachers actually disdain their counterparts who give greater credence to the affective elements. The more creative teachers seem to have the same impatience with those who prefer an analytic approach to the task. Affective approaches are considered to be lightweight and unworthy.[4] Cognitive approaches are thought to be stuffy and uninspiring.[5]

4. "Stories have emotional impact, but they are lightweight compared with Scripture. . . . In my mind, stories tend to shut down the level of intensity that I prefer people to maintain. I tell a story when it is appropriate, but this happens only rarely." John MacArthur Jr., *Rediscovering Expository Preaching: Balancing the Science and Art of Biblical Exposition* (Dallas: Word, 1992), 342–43.

5. "You study hard all week, do your exegesis, apply all the rules of hermeneutics, and come up with a lot of helpful biblical material that you want your congregation to know. You organize it on your homiletical 'conveyor belt' and as soon as the choir finishes its anthem, you throw the switch and start the belt moving. All of this marvelous material passes from the pulpit to the pew and the worshipers are supposed to pick it up and make it their own. But it just doesn't

This bifurcated and adversarial thinking ought to be self-evidentially narrow, perhaps even bigoted in its partiality and intolerance toward the other. If this language of prejudice seems harsh, it is only because few of us actually see ourselves in such *dis*integrated fashion. When seen in distinction, it ought to seem ridiculous that we would be so dismissive of the capacities that God has implanted in us.

Simply put, to paint a picture is not detrimental to the exegesis of a word. A picture might be worth a thousand words, but every one of those words captures significant meaning. Saint Francis is thought to have said that we should preach the gospel to everyone—and if necessary that we would use words. The truth is that it is always necessary to use our words. The effects of the gospel are as numerous as they are beautiful, but the gospel is unintelligible and powerless without the words that give it definition.

Francis himself knew this. While he no doubt expressed his message through his life and influence, he was also unafraid to use his words. Francis was prolific, offering five or six sermons per day as he traveled from village to village. Of the many words he spoke, it may surprise us to learn that those words for which he is credited probably never passed his lips. There is no record that he ever suggested that the gospel could be preached without a corresponding use of words. For Francis, words and pictures—head and heart—were fully integrated.[6]

This is how we live our lives. Whenever we buy a computer or a cell phone, few of us consult the manuals before attempting operation. A famous 1980s-era advertisement for Apple computers displayed a stack of instruction manuals several inches deep, necessary for the understanding and operation of an IBM computer. The Apple manual, by contrast, was only a few pages in length. The image required very little exposition. Apple computers required less instruction to operate. They were designed to "plug and play"—no complicated explanation required.

These days, this is the way we manage most technologies. If manuals exist at all, they are offered online and not packaged with the item. We simply unpack our toys and start messing around. When we run into trouble, we go to the web and find the help we need. This experience is ubiquitous, which raises the question: If this uninstructed way is the manner of our lives, might it be the manner of our preaching?

Well, no, because a mere experience of grace is not enough for a full and faithful mastery of the gospel. We would not argue for an ignorant faith,

---

work that way." Warren W. Wiersbe, *Preaching and Teaching with Imagination: The Quest for Biblical Ministry* (Grand Rapids: Baker, 1994), 20.

6. Mark Galli, "Speak the Gospel: Use Deeds When Necessary," *Christianity Today*, May 21, 2009, http://www.christianitytoday.com/ct/2009/mayweb-only/120-42.0.html.

managed solely through intuitive conception. We would, at the same time, not want to embrace a faith paralyzed through analysis, imperiled by a lack of heart.

Paul's Appeal to Philippian Hearts and Minds

In Philippians 4:7 Paul encourages the guarding of his friends' hearts and minds in Christ Jesus. It is the combination of the two elements that makes Paul's encouragement so compelling.

It is interesting to imagine, for example, the heart without the mind, or the mind without the heart. Which organ provides the physical core of human life? A brain separated from its body cannot long function without the lifeblood supplied by the pumping heart. The heart, without a brain to guide its function, lies inert and useless to any purpose on the earth. The heart empowers the mind. The mind directs the heart. One requires the other for the body to meet its purpose.

Biblically speaking, the two terms are used almost interchangeably. The mind (*nous*) in Scripture describes a person's mental processes or, more broadly, the totality of one's mental state of being. The heart (*kardia*), similarly, is the biblical center of a person's being. The expression serves as shorthand for a person's character, will, and being. It is almost impossible to read the terms *dis*integrated if we are to read the Bible right.

Paul addresses disunity within the Philippian church, encouraging his two friends Euodia and Syntyche to a more agreeable way of being (Phil. 4). He encourages them to rejoice (heart) and to be reasonable (mind). He encourages them on the affective level, suggesting that it is the peace of God that will guard their hearts and minds, but then immediately challenges them to more appropriate cognitive patterns, to think on things that are true and just and noble. He offers himself as a personal example: "Whatever you have learned or received or heard from me [head], or seen in me [heart]—put it into practice. And the God of peace will be with you" (v. 9). The rejoicing that brings peace is valued as highly as the thinking that roots a person in the truth.

In fact, this integrated emphasis runs throughout the entire book. In the opening verses of Philippians, Paul speaks of how he longs "for all of [them] with the affection of Christ Jesus" (1:8). It is his deep desire that their love might abound more and more, but not in some unbridled, thoughtless way, but "in knowledge and depth of insight" (1:9). It is a considered love he counsels, feelings disciplined by thought.

In Philippians 3:10 Paul describes his paramount longing to know Christ. But this is not a knowledge limited to cognitive understanding. Paul longs for something much more visceral. He wants to share in the sufferings of Christ. He is willing to become like Christ in his death. He wants to attain, even, to the resurrection from the dead. It is hard to imagine a more integrated aspiration.

Indeed, it is in the resurrection that the integration of head and heart is seen in its most perfect and compelling expression. In Philippians 2:10 Paul describes the ultimate and eventual result of Christ's incarnation—that every knee will bow and every tongue confess that Jesus Christ is Lord. The confession of the tongue is the perfected expression of the mind. The bowing of the knee is the ideal expression of the will. Head and heart find ultimate congruence in the presence of Christ in the moment when the earth is finally functioning at its created optimum. Tongues and knees display the integration of heads and hearts when all is exactly as everything should be.

Thoughts and Feelings of the Cross

This is the intention of the cross. Jesus himself taught and embodied wisdom, but he also embraced joy and sorrow as one who lived a fully human life. Jesus was appreciated not only for what he said but also for how he said it. The cross not only achieved forensic justification, satisfying the penalty that sin required, but it also offered emotional catharsis, expressing the cosmic relief of a world released from groaning.

You can see that Jesus feels it on the cross. "My God, my God," he wails, fully writhing in the pain of divine abandonment. The weight of sin was crushing as he came to know the deep and darkest horror of human depravity. Every instance of prideful deceit, domestic abuse, lustful abandon, thieving disregard—every malfeasance ever visited on planet Earth came to be paid on his account in that single moment. The pain and the pathos of his experience are beyond imagination.

Yet at the same time Jesus knows—he knows exactly what must happen in that moment. He knows that sin must be satisfied and that it will find satisfaction as the sinless one puts paid to our account. In that moment, Jesus is a theologian. He has done the intellectual math, understanding that his calculated action is what is necessary for the reconciliation of all creation. This is a thoughtful, deliberative moment. In fact, without this deliberative conviction, there is no way he can embrace the pain the act delivers. Sin brings suffering. It is and was *excruciating*—etymologically, "out of the cross" (ex-crux)—and Jesus felt every bit of it. There is a reason that we describe this as "the passion."

The result was our salvation. The created purpose of the universe was restored and set to right by the action of the cross. It is required that we respond with celebration. Worship is more than just the development of right conviction. Worship is the converse of excruciation. The pain of the cross is overcome by the worship made possible by the result achieved. It ought to be exuberant. The cross brings together head and heart. It is a body of knowledge even as it is a reason for our joy.

How Integration Helps in Life

Christian people are called to follow the way of the cross in how we manage our lives. Through cross-formed integration, each element of our life and faith fulfills the other. For example, our feelings can be brought in conformity with the truth by thoughtful examination. We all know what it is like to wake up on the wrong side of the bed in the morning. Our feelings, when disconnected from the truths that govern our existence, can lead to discouraged and depressive states. It is important that we always check what we feel with what we know. Truth needs to discipline emotion so that we are not driven by feelings that have gone rogue.

On that morning when we rise disagreeably, it can be helpful to rehearse the truths that constitute our faith. We know that God loves us and that this love cannot be thwarted by anything in the universe. We know that we have been created on purpose, and that purpose extends the things we have to do along the trajectory that governs the entire universe. We know that we have been forgiven for our sin and that our position in Christ is secure. We know that we are, then, free and unencumbered by the dysfunctional assessments put on us by others. Getting our head in order can go a long way toward getting our heart in order so that our day is governed by the things that are true and not by the winds that come and go in culture.

The reverse is also true. We know what it is to let our thoughts deflate us—to think ourselves into ever-encroaching circles so that our thoughts tie us in knots. Sometimes this is the result of poor thinking, unwarranted thoughts that confound and lead us only deeper into ourselves. But even truthful thinking can starve us if these thoughts are not allowed to live and breathe.

Theologically, we describe the Scriptures as "inspired by God." Typically, we see this as speaking to the authority of the Bible and its expression of cognitive and objective truth. It would help us to remember that the word *inspire* comes from the sense that God has "breathed" his Word (2 Tim. 3:16). The Word of God is the very breath of God. It comes from inside him. It is the animating essence of God that fills, enlivens, and "inflates" us.

When we find our thoughts turning in on themselves and we feel lost or even stymied by the depth of our concerns, it is helpful for us to lean in the direction of the heart. It helps us to remember that truth has a capital *T*. Truth does not only describe the conceptual nature of God. God is a person, and Truth is his name. To know truth is to know God and to be filled by him. Engaging the heart empowers the value of what the mind knows.

This is one value of worship, where we act with intention to appreciate and sense the glory of God and the presence of his Spirit. Intentionally going out of doors so as to experience creation can be a life-giving tonic expanding our appreciation for the truth we understand. Engaging in community or being with our family gives us opportunity to see how truth can be enfleshed in the relationships that give our thoughts a context. Putting ourselves in positions where our hearts can speak to our heads is part of how we might be formed.

Communicating to and through Both Head and Heart

As communicators who care about the formation of another's soul, we will want to find ways to speak both to the head and to the heart. A person cannot live by instruction alone, and more than inspiration is needed also. We need the words to go with the music, the caption to bring meaning to the picture.

The goal is to embrace both *logos* and *pathos*.[7] Aristotle understood that our talk is credited by the information that gives warrant to our claims, but that when that information is addressed with appropriate emotion, the impact is much greater. We need to understand the technical schematics, but we might not be convinced until we see the artist's rendering.

Great communicators are careful to explain even as they passionately inspire, in keeping with the best of learning theory. Educational theorist David Kolb is famous for his experiential learning model, wherein he describes "the thinkers" (characterized by "reflective observation") and "the feelers" (focused on "active experimentation").[8] Kolb's concern is that we need to speak integratively to both. It is a case of the result being greater than the sum of the parts. "Integrative learning," he writes, "occurs when two or more elementary forms

7. Patricia Bizze and Bruce Herzberg, *The Rhetorical Tradition: Readings from Classical Times to the Present* (Boston: Bedford Books of St. Martin's, 1990), 29.

8. David A. Kolb, *Experiential Learning: Experience as the Source of Learning and Development* (Englewood Cliffs, NJ: Prentice-Hall, 1984), 67–69.

of learning combine to produce a higher-order integration of the elementary differentiations around their common learning mode(s)."[9]

Kolb uses the example of an automotive museum in which one encounters a beautiful car without an engine. In another part of the museum there is an engine separate from the vehicle. It is in the unity of the two that one finds an exponential power.[10]

We may find that we have a natural way of leaning, either in the direction of the mind or more toward the heart. Some of us are naturally creative thinkers, and others gravitate toward critical thinking. These orientations can feel as natural to us as any other defining characteristic. We display these ways from birth, moving naturally in the direction of education and experience that only deepens and confirms these initial propensities.

This is true, of course, for every human listener who comes to hear us speak. If our talk leans in the direction of our own inclination, we will typically attract those who are wired like we are. This will likely allow us to feel good about ourselves, as the environment will seem affirming. Highly cognitive preachers will naturally attract thinkers. Highly affective preachers will more normally attract creatives. But if we care about mission and about reaching the whole of our communities, we will want to move beyond what comes easiest to us. As committed communicators, the onus is on us to do what we must to help our listeners hear. We will speak both to the head and to the heart. In so doing, we will embrace more of what is expected of us, reaching a greater breadth of people, and reveal more of the nature of God himself.

Sheldon Vanauken, a friend of C. S. Lewis, came to appreciate this early in his life. As a boy, he found he had a natural affinity for books and for intellectual learning. Beauty, for him, was incomprehensible. He had no category for this. Remembering this period in his life, he writes:

> He remembered as though it were but a few days ago that winter night, himself too young even to know the meaning of beauty, when he had looked up at a delicate tracery of bare black branches against the icy glittering stars: suddenly something that was, all at once, pain and longing and adoring had welled up in him, almost choking him. He had wanted to tell someone, but he had no words, inarticulate in the pain and glory. It was long afterwards that he realized that this had been his first aesthetic experience. That nameless something that had stopped his heart was Beauty.[11]

9. Ibid., 146.
10. Ibid.
11. "And of course beauty: the beauty was the thing for him the link between the ships and the woods and poems. . . . He remembered suddenly a particular summer morning, wandering about the woodlands with Polly. . . . He had been wont to despise emotions: girls were emotional,

Vanauken's book *A Severe Mercy* is a love story, the account of the life and death of his beloved wife, Davy, and their mutual growth to know and appreciate the love of God. It is not in error that he capitalized *Beauty*, for he came to know that aesthetic truth is as much a part of the character of God as intellectual Truth. To know God is to be loved by him—to feel his presence even as we come to appreciate his mind.

The horizontal line describes this integrative way of being in physical terms. Both our cognitive functions (head) and our affective responses (heart) play out across this horizontal groundedness. Physically, we think and feel and have our being.

---

girls were weak, emotions—tears—were weakness. But this morning he was thinking that being a great brain in a tower, nothing but a brain, wouldn't be much fun." Sheldon Vanauken, *A Severe Mercy* (New York: Harper & Row, 1977), 16–17. Years later, James K. A. Smith wrote similarly of this "brain in a tower" concept: "The result is a talking-head version of Christianity that is fixated in doctrines and ideas, even if it is paradoxically allied with a certain kind of anti-intellectualism. We could describe this as a 'bobble-head' Christianity, so fixated on the cognitive that it assumes a picture of human beings that look like bobble heads: mammoth heads that dwarf an almost non-existent body." James K. A. Smith, *Desiring the Kingdom: Worship, Worldview, and Cultural Formation* (Grand Rapids: Baker Academic, 2009), 42–43.

3

Preaching Is Vertical (Spiritual)

The cover of U2's 2009 album, *No Line on the Horizon*, features a striking photograph by Japanese artist Hiroshi Sugimoto. The photo, titled *Boden Sea*, is a picture of Lake Constance, an alpine lake in Switzerland. Evenly dividing the gray sky from the even darker gray sea, the album art depicts a perfectly flat horizon. The band had in mind "a place where the sea meets the sky and the sky meets the sea and you cannot tell the difference."[1] It is a place where there is no horizon—no line dividing heaven and earth, where the only definition is vertical—a place where heaven and human find integration.

This is U2 picking up their Celtic heritage. The Celts love to speak of "thin places," physical locations that speak so eloquently to the presence of God that there seems little or no separation between heaven and earth—places where there is no line on the horizon.

N. T. Wright has picked up on this theme, suggesting that individual Christians actualize these thin places, serving as personal points of contact between heaven and earth. As those who live in Christ, believers embody the touch of heaven to the earth. The goal of the Christian, according to Wright, is to extend these points of contact such that these horizonless zones spread larger and larger on the earth.[2]

1. Brad Frenette, "U2's No Line on the Horizon: A Track-by-Track Exclusive with Producer/Co-Writer Daniel Lanois," *National Post*, March 10, 2009, http://www.webcitation.org/5kfqFaK30.

2. "The renewal and reclaiming of *space* has recently involved, among other things, a fresh grasp of the Celtic tradition of 'thin places,' places where the curtain between heaven and earth

The integrative life sustains the value of the horizontal while making space for the vertical line, the spiritual axis that defines the distance between heaven and human, the objective and the subjective, integrating the possibility of both.

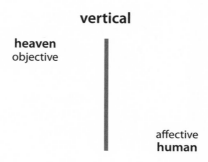

vertical

heaven
objective

affective
human

Earth Is Not Enough

It is in the integration of the horizontal and the vertical that we find the essence of the gospel. The horizontal line is intersected by the vertical meridian. Heaven meets earth as God comes down in the person of his Son. The gospel begins with a statement of our current reality. We live our lives on planet Earth, and yet we know *the earth is not enough*. This is the horizontal line. Subject to gravity, we spread ourselves across the planet. We live across the horizontal plane, and yet all along we know that it is not enough, nor will it ever be.

We live with restrictions measured to us by our bodies. Our reach is limited to what we can touch and what we can see, what we can build and what we can buy. The laws of physics determine how far we can go and how fast we can get there. The substance of our available resources limits our opportunities. It is frustrating. We travel, we study, we invest, and with every bit of knowledge gained, we are only more aware of what we cannot reach. The more we know, the more we know we will never know.

We understand only what we have seen or what we have experienced. We sense that the universe offers us a greater substance, but we cannot aspire to what we do not know or cannot imagine. We marshal the smartest among us to think deep thoughts, mining the possibilities of a horizontal life, but it is not enough. The earth is not enough. It never could be.

_____

seems almost transparent." N. T. Wright, *Surprised by Hope: Rethinking Heaven, the Resurrection, and the Mission of the Church* (New York: HarperOne, 2008), 259.

Heaven Is beyond Us

We know that we were built for more than just an earthbound life. There is something innate within us that stretches and searches for more than all we have. We long for more, but *heaven is beyond us*.

The tallest among us cannot reach to the heavens. The strongest and the wisest are insufficient for our infinite ambition. We know we have potential— that there is something bred in us that grasps for something greater. We just can't reach it on our own. Our arms are not long enough, our capacity insufficient for the things that we have craved.

We look to the heavens, and what we see astounds us. The heavens declare the glory of God, the psalmist says (Ps. 19:1). But this God seems inaccessible to us, precisely because of his glory. It is above and beyond the scope of our ambition.

Star Trek describes space as "the final frontier," wherein we find our mission "to explore strange new worlds, to seek out new life and new civilizations, to boldly go where no man has gone before." This vision still compels us, as the ever-expanding list of *Star Trek* titles will attest, even as funding for actual manned space exploration seems to be drying up. The mission of the *Enterprise* was adapted from a White House pamphlet encouraging space exploration that was published in 1958. Almost sixty years later, we have come to see these stories of Vulcans, Klingons, and strange new worlds as the stuff of fantasy—diversionary subjects for costume play but not for serious consideration.

It is deeply frustrating, given that a desire for heaven or God, or at least for some sense of transcendence, seems hardwired into the genetic code of human life—if not literally, then at least as aspiration. People seem to be naturally inclined toward the metaphysical, which is surprising given our lack of access to it. Our human insistence on eternity is countered by our deep experience with death. Electrocardiogram machines depict a healthy life as a series of ups and downs—a jagged line across the horizon. A flat line indicates death, which seems appropriate given how we long for a life that can exceed the limits of the merely physical.

We try to "get vertical," climbing the highest mountains in order to somehow approach the heavens with a greater sense of immediacy, yet the higher we climb, the thinner the air and the more dangerous the terrain. The probability of death increases the higher we go, which only seems to drive us higher in our quest. Jon Krakauer is perhaps the most eloquent in his description of this phenomenon. "I quickly came to understand," he says, "that climbing Everest was primarily about enduring pain. And in subjecting ourselves to week after week of toil, tedium, and suffering, it struck me that most of us were probably seeking, above else, something like a state of grace."[3]

Robert Browning put it well when he said, "A man's reach should exceed his grasp, / Or what's a heaven for?"[4] This is the kind of tortured yearning one might expect of a nineteenth-century poet—beautifully expressed, but not of much help. What kind of answer is it that our most profound ambition would exceed our grasp?

God Brought Heaven Down to Earth

It would be a cruel joke, were it not for the fact that *God brought heaven down to earth*. The vertical line of the cross, drawn from the top down, represents this truth. God, by deliberate action, made it possible for those he created to exceed their physical limitations by bringing heaven down to earth:

1. Earth is not enough.
2. Heaven is beyond us.
3. God brought heaven down to earth.

Theologically, we call this "incarnation." It is the act by which God made himself flesh and dwelt among us in the person of Jesus Christ. The nickname of Jesus is "Immanuel," which means "God with us." Focused on his intention for creation, God acted decisively to do for us what we could not do for ourselves. He transcended the gap between heaven and earth. He made himself known to us by becoming one with us. Speaking our language and living our lives, he made it possible for us to relate to him.

Of course, this relationship required a deeper kind of personal engagement. Not only did God need to make himself present to us, but also he had to solve the problem of our sin. Having succumbed to the presence of sin, the earth was cursed to decay and death, with all of humankind under the subsequent sentence of eternal death.

We have become accustomed to this reality, such that we hardly conceive of anything beyond our death. Death is the realest thing we know, leading us to a pragmatic, take-what-we-can-get-while-we-can-get-it approach to life on

3. Jon Krakauer, *Into Thin Air: A Personal Account of the Mount Everest Disaster* (New York: Anchor Books, 1997), 140.

4. Robert Browning, "Andrea del Sarto," Poetry Foundation, accessed November 30, 2016, http://www.poetryfoundation.org/poems-and-poets/poems/detail/43745.

earth. We have forgotten that the separation of heaven from earth was not part of the original design.

We were created to know and be in fellowship with God. Originally, God walked on the earth. Eden was heavenly—the display of Jesus's prayer that the kingdom would be known on earth as it is in heaven. Sin put an end to that, breaking faith with the Creator. Sin was humanity's way of asserting its independence from God. It was the expression of our rebellion—our desire to master ourselves. The separation of heaven from earth was of our own doing and by our choice.

We have never been much comfortable with that choice. By choosing to manage our own lives, we have divorced ourselves from the possibility of a heaven.[5] Yet we have never been able to escape the sense that we have lost something essential in the bargain. Death is the enemy against which we rage. We do not go gentle into that good night, because we can't abide the fact of our mortality.[6] We were created for heaven, whether we wish to acknowledge it or not, yet we have to live on earth—subject to gravity and accountable to death. There is nothing we can do to save ourselves from this reality, beyond trying to establish an influence that lives after us. Heaven is beyond us, and there is nothing that *we* can do for it.

Which is why the solution had to be at God's initiative. God brought heaven down to earth. God acted on our behalf in a top-down action. He made the vertical move to insert himself among us and to ultimately pay the price for our sin. The death of Jesus was the compensatory act necessary to atone for our sin. With sin forgiven, the distance between heaven and earth has been overcome.

It is significant that in the final chapters of the Bible, heaven is pictured as a city that vertically descends, merging with the renewed earth (Rev. 21:1–2). The ultimate end of all things offers a perfected integration of "the new heaven" with "the new earth." God has brought heaven down to earth such that we can know him and live on earth as it is in heaven.

The Integration of the Objective and the Subjective

Integrative preaching requires this vertical axis—the integration of heaven and earth, of the object and the subject. We have long understood the difference between objective truth and subjective experience. Theologically,

---

5. C. S. Lewis, *The Great Divorce* (New York: MacMillan, 1946), v.
6. Dylan Thomas, "Do Not Go Gentle into That Good Night," Poets.org, accessed November 30, 2016, https://www.poets.org/poetsorg/poem/do-not-go-gentle-good-night.

we appreciate the idea that the Creator as the originator is definitively objective, while the creation is literally subjective—subject to the will of the Creator. Given that we are locked in space and time, we despair of reaching anything beyond our subjectivity. Postmodern philosophers remind us that even if we were to grasp something objective, we would immediately stain it with our fingerprints.[7] Our subjectivity is voracious, swallowing anything objective we might touch. This is because everything we experience is perceived from our place in space and time. Everything we "know" is viewed through the glass of our experience, our education, and our passions. We can know nothing that we have not shaped in some way for our own purposes.

Not that this is a bad thing. Some of us have sensed that the only thing of value in the universe is objective truth, and this is for good reason. It is worshipful and it is truthful to reserve for God absolute and ultimate worth. God must be Other or he cannot be God. A world without the possibility of truth is a world that lacks a center. Without a center, the world could not cohere—it could not hold.

But it is just as important to acknowledge that people in space and time must appropriate truth—they must take hold of it. Truth that remains pure and abstracted from the experience of people on the earth is not helpful to God's purposes. Truth must touch us, and if it is ruffled by the touch, it is no less true. The cross itself was grounded in the rocky soil of Calvary. Jesus's sacrifice was true because it was real.

This is why it is helpful for people like you and me to talk about this. Not only do human preachers and teachers embody and endorse the truth by their speaking of it. It is important that we give voice to the truth so that it finds its place and takes its shape on earth.

On Earth as It Is in Heaven

Jesus was among the first to speak and preach about an earthly kingdom. This was, in fact, the core message of his famous Sermon on the Mount. Jesus's sermon comprises three chapters, Matthew 5, 6, and 7. The centerpiece of the sermon is Jesus's model prayer, found halfway through the middle chapter. The prayer begins with the call for God's kingdom to be realized "on earth as it is in heaven" (Matt. 6:10). This expression serves as shorthand for the entire sermon.

7. G. B. Madison, *The Hermeneutics of Postmodernity: Figures and Themes* (Bloomington: Indiana University Press, 1988), 9.

Jesus describes how we can begin to live the values and intentions of heaven while still living here on earth. He is teaching how we can become personal hot spots where heaven touches earth. As N. T. Wright suggests, we learn from Jesus how to extend the influence of heaven, spreading heaven's way across the earth as we live and move and have our being.[8] In some small way we are actualizing the prayer of Jesus, that the kingdom would be expressed on earth just as it is in heaven until he comes to fully and finally consummate his plan.

In chapter 5 Jesus describes how this works in terms of how we relate to one another. In chapter 6 he describes what this looks like in relationship with him. The seventh chapter plays both out in fuller detail.

Chapter 5 lays out a contrast between the law of heaven and the law of earth. The law of earth, with its codes and statutes, regulates the physical manner of our lives. The earth is crowded. We bump into each other a lot. The law provides a means of managing our conflict. As long as we live here on earth, we require the law, and Jesus understood that. "I have not come to abolish them [the Law or the Prophets]," he says in verse 17, "but to fulfill them."

Heaven has a different operating system. Heaven represents the purest and most objective form of life intended for us in creation. The law of heaven is not judicial or punitive. It describes, rather, the way of being compelled by an unrestricted sense of the presence of a loving and all-wise God.

The law of heaven completes the original intention for the law in that it describes the way that created humans were originally intended to live and be. The law, as a disciplining force on earth, restricts the spread of evil and encourages ways of doing life that are more and more in congruence with the law of heaven.[9]

Throughout the fifth chapter, Jesus lays out a parallel structure that juxtaposes the law of heaven and the law of earth. Six times he offers us the structure: "You have heard that it was said, but I tell you . . ." The "you have heard that it was said" part refers to the law as we know it here on earth. "But I tell you . . ." is where he describes the fulfillment of the law of heaven. In each case, the second clause elevates and perfects the intention of the first. It is the way that Jesus actualizes his fulfillment of the law of earth.

He begins, for example, by supporting our legal prohibition against murder. This is a good law—so good that it is still on the books in every civilized country on the earth. When we find ourselves in serious conflict, murder is not an appropriate solution, as it is an egregious infringement on the right

8. Wright, *Surprised by Hope*, 112.

9. Dallas Willard, *The Divine Conspiracy: Rediscovering Our Hidden Life with God* (San Francisco: HarperSanFrancisco, 1998), 146–47.

of the other—the right to live. Only God himself has the authority to give or take human life. So we prohibit murder by law, and everyone agrees that this is as it should be. Jesus himself affirms and supports the law against murder.

But Jesus doesn't leave it there. It is not sufficient that we simply do not kill each other. As citizens of the kingdom of heaven, we must not even want to. "But I tell you that anyone who is angry with a brother or sister will be subject to judgment" (v. 22). He continues to teach that even to think a brother foolish or to hold him in contempt is a violation of the law of heaven.[10] Don't kill each other, Jesus says. That is a good way of handling life on earth. But as citizens of the heavenly kingdom, you should not even nurture the desire.

"You have heard that it was said, 'You shall not commit adultery'" (v. 27). This remains a good idea to this day, though most nations have determined to leave it as a matter of social and not legal jurisdiction. We would manage better in the world if we could respect our commitments in marriage.

"But I tell you that anyone who looks at a woman lustfully has already committed adultery with her in his heart" (v. 28). Clearly, this has taken things to another level—the level of the law of heaven. In heaven, what we do with our bodies (or what can be regulated by the law of earth) is not the only thing at issue. In heaven the law extends from our external actions to the actions of our heart. In heaven, what we do with our heart matters as much as what we do with our hands and with our feet.

This level of concern challenges us beyond what is normally considered to be reasonable. The Philip Dick story (and Tom Cruise movie) *Minority Report* describes a time in future history where the law is able to reach to the level of "pre-crime." In this world, accountability and prosecution extend not just to what is done but to what is merely planned or intended. While such a system might be helpful in protecting victims from crimes not yet committed, it seems an unreasonable reach to punish people for what they had only thought about. Yet Jesus's law takes things even further than Philip Dick imagined. The law of heaven is concerned not just with what has been done or what might be intended but with what is intellectually indulged. The incident might not ever become physical for it to be damaging.

I saw this illustrated in a Michael Douglas movie, *It Runs in the Family*. Douglas portrays a successful businessman who is trying hard to be a good man. He volunteers at a soup kitchen under the direction of an attractive woman who decides she would like to seduce him. He resists her temptation not because he isn't interested but because he doesn't want to be a bad guy. He wants to be a good man. This woman, however, is not so easily dissuaded.

10. Ibid., 151–54.

A few days later, Douglas's wife is searching for her husband's cell phone in the pockets of his overcoat. There she finds a pair of women's underwear, placed there by the other woman, unbeknownst to him. "I didn't do it," he protests. "I would not do this. I am not that kind of man!"

"All right," his wife says. "I believe you. You didn't do it." Dramatic pause. "But did you want to?"

Did he want to? Of course he wanted to. It is all he has been able to think about for days. But he did not do this thing, and for him that was the important factor. For his wife, however, this betrayal of the heart was every bit as damaging as if he had done the physical deed.

This is Jesus's point exactly. We might not be able to regulate by law the ways of our hearts and minds on earth, but such regulation is the way of things within the realm of heaven. The law of heaven affects not just whether we are speaking truth but whether we are people who have truthful hearts. The law of heaven goes beyond whether or not we have done damage to our enemy to whether or not we have love for them. The law of heaven indicates not just whether we have logged minutes and hours in prayer but whether that prayer accurately reflects the inner nature of our heart and will. The law of heaven is concerned not about the spiritual persona we present to others but about whether we are attentive to the Spirit on the level of the heart. This is what it means to be a tree that bears good fruit—to build a structure on a solid foundation.

This is what it looks like to see the kingdom come on earth as it is in heaven.

The Effect of the Cross on Heaven and Earth

Cross-formed preaching is about the integration of heaven and earth. The achievement of the cross has these two dimensions: eternal salvation and physical re-creation. Jesus's work on the cross was sufficient for the eternal salvation of all those who place faith in him and in what he has done. Jesus Christ, the sinless one, took on flesh and blood to make God accessible to us physically and also spiritually. By resolving the problem that sin presents regarding our relationship with a holy God, Jesus made it possible for us to be reconciled to God. The cross renewed the terms of our relationship with God, putting paid to our sin for all eternity.

But there is another dimension to what the cross achieves. The Bible describes the way that sin has cursed the physical earth. Sin brought to the earth a sense of toil and strife. Thorns and thistles came to represent the earth's subjectivity to decay (Gen. 3:17). The earth became a dying place, slowly and inexorably. Our current debates about climate causation and human agency betray a deeper cause. Human sin brought death to the earth, and all creation groans, awaiting its redemption (Rom. 8:22).

Which is why it is so encouraging to read to the end of the New Testament to see that God has more in mind for the earth he has created. We do not await the destruction of the earth. We anticipate the re-creation of the earth. The revelation is of "a new heaven and a new earth" as the heavenly city integrates with the re-created earth (Rev. 21:1). The effect of the cross is not a repudiation of the earth but a perfection of it as the objective and the subjective are properly and perfectly integrated for all time.

The Preaching of the Cross

And this, again, is both the subject and the manner of our preaching. Preaching the cross is preaching that crosses the objective and subjective domains, bringing ultimate truth to bear on immediate concerns. Our goal is not to speak solely of heavenly things such that "the things of life grow strangely dim." The objective of our talking is that we might fully and finally see the earth more clearly.

Whenever I hear a worship leader invite me to let go of all bothersome thought of life in order to focus my thoughts entirely on Jesus, I am not sure what to do. Thinking of an abstract Jesus is not particularly helpful. I do not see Jesus in some disembodied spiritual state. I see Jesus in the way that he has showed himself to me—with a body, the Son of God and the Son of Man. My goal is not to see Jesus apart from my concern for the things of this world. My desire is to bring these things to Jesus so that he can renovate them.

In another of God's acts of condescension (descending to be with us), the Holy Spirit came down to earth. Earth is the venue for the Spirit's action. Our worship, then, ought not to be Platonic. It ought to sweat and breathe—and so must our speaking of it.

We observed how David Kolb, in his discussion of learning styles, spoke of the "thinkers" and the "feelers" (head and heart). But he also spoke of the "watchers" and the "doers." More specifically, he spoke of the distinction between "abstract conceptualization" (what the watchers value) and "concrete experience" (what the doers value).[11] The challenge in education and in persuasive communication, according to Kolb, is to speak to both. Bringing together all four of Kolb's learning styles—watching, doing, thinking, and

---

11. David A. Kolb, *Experiential Learning: Experience as the Source of Learning and Development* (Englewood Cliffs, NJ: Prentice-Hall, 1984), 67–69.

feeling—is a way of talking that has integrity. Thus, it offers the most compelling opportunity for a preferred future, though perhaps not the safest. "Integrative knowing is essentially eclectic. . . . It stands with one foot in the canoe of an emergent future—a most uncomfortable and taxing position, one that positively demands commitment to either forging ahead or jumping back to safety."[12]

Those with the courage to adopt this integrative posture will have the most compelling things to say.

God Uses Humans in His Preaching

We often wonder why God might need us in his service. God is capable of speaking for himself. Why is it necessary for human beings to speak on his behalf? How is it even possible for us to offer the word of truth without messing it up, either by our sin or by our physical limitations? Human speakers are prideful people. When things go poorly, we despair—we cannot see beyond the immediate disappointment. When things go well, we tend to take the credit, as if it were our personal brilliance or eloquence that achieves the things of God.

And yet the human element in preaching, flawed for the moment, actually empowers the integration we have been speaking of. A human person talks about the incarnate Christ by means of the inspired Word, under the power of the indwelling Spirit. It is, of course, a vertical, top-down movement. Such talk is always dependent on God's grace. We may be essentially engaged, but it is always the work of God, driven by his eternal love for us.

It is a joyful thing that we get to be a part of it—that we must be a part of it. By this strange and wonderful integration, ultimate truth is spoken into human space, on earth as it is in heaven—no line on the horizon.

---

12. Ibid., 225.

4

Preaching Is Centripetal (Kinetic)

I remember the first time I rode the Gravitron. More science experiment than amusement-park ride, the Gravitron utilizes centrifugal force to generate a thrill. It was hard to know exactly what to expect when I stepped onto the ride. There were no cars—it was not going to take me anywhere. Still, the excitement was palpable. I was strapped into place around the inside circumference of a large bowl. The bowl was then set into motion and accelerated until I was fully flattened against the wall at my back. I could not move. I was absolutely motionless. The force was overwhelming. If it wasn't for the steel wall at my back, I would have been propelled backward like a bullet from a gun.

This physical phenomenon pictures the effect of the integrative model. Centrifugal force exists only in a state of significant rotational movement. It has no effect within an inertial state of being. But when the centrifuge is set in motion, dense materials within the field are propelled outward and away. The movement outward *dis*integrates, separating and pulling apart everything that had been drawn together. Centrifugal force is the enemy of integration.

Centripetal Force

Centripetal force describes the opposite effect, pulling strong toward an anchored center point, with everything finding unity at the center. Consider, for example, a stone being whirled around on a string.[1] The force acting on

1. F. Bueche, *Principles of Physics*, 3rd ed. (New York: McGraw-Hill, 1977), 143.

the stone is the tension in the string. There is no force on the stone itself. The string holds the stone in a kind of orbit, tracing a circle around the center point, resisting the force that wants to send the object outward. It is that anchored center that pulls everything toward the middle.

In the integrative preaching model, the horizontal overlays the vertical to create a centered cross-point. As the sermon moves, head is pulled toward heart, and heaven is drawn toward the human, as the whole thing converges toward the cross-point. The centripetal force exerted on a sermon creates a similar sense of integrative unity as the elements overlap and interact around the cross. It is motion that keeps the tension on the string. A state of inertia has no force. The sermon has to move for it to have its impact. It has to take us somewhere.

Inertia is the natural tendency of an object to resist changes in its state of motion. Inertia is resistant, not restful. It may describe a settled state of being, but that settledness is itself resistant to the movement that our soul requires. If things don't move, they become stagnant. If we settle in our soul, we are actually resisting the movement of the Spirit—the things that God has put in motion.

We naturally resist the motion that might lead us toward productive change. Motion sickness occurs whenever there is disagreement between what one sees visually and what one experiences internally. This is a good metaphor for what happens to us when we try to lock into a settled place while the world keeps moving. We get sick—spiritually ill. When we stop looking and listening, when our vision dies so that what we are seeing is out of sync with what God is doing in our heart, we experience a kind of spiritual motion sickness.

Our habitual inertia works against the things that God expects to do in us—the change intended by the cross. It is impossible to steer a parked vehicle, but put that vehicle in motion and a direction can be charted. The sermon also wants to move. It yearns to have a cross-formed purpose. Preaching ought not to settle into the comfort of instruction without the resultant inspiration. It must not be content to be engaging unless it also moves toward conviction.

The world is in motion because God himself is in motion. That God is eternal does not mean that he is not active. God is at work. There is a trajectory to history. The world and all that is within is moving toward God's eternal purpose. That purpose has culminated in the cross. When we preach, we embrace that purpose. Our proclamation places us within the flow of movement God has propelled.

The integrative model of preaching is built on a set of *elements* and *compounds*. The elements are the essential functions of the preaching task. The compounds are the materials that result when the elements are integrated.

These compound materials make up the substance of the preacher's speaking. Through the preacher's use of these materials, the elemental functions of the sermon are produced.

The Functional Elements of Integrative Preaching

The preacher's goal is to lead the listener on a journey through the elements of preaching. The sermon begins with the human at the bottom of the cross. This is where the cross sinks down into the earthy ground of human life. First, the sermon must *engage*. The preacher has to find the listener where she lives, engaging the reality of life on the ground. Our sermons must be human before they can be heavenly.

Next, the sermon must *instruct*, the second element of integrative preaching. This is the left side of the cross, where the sermon extends itself intellectually to embrace the head—the transformation of the listener's mind. Humans need not be empty-headed in their engagement with their God.

Now the sermon is in motion, beginning to exert its centripetal force. Engagement leads to instruction, leading next toward conviction as the sermon gains momentum. Instruction must *convict*, the third sermonic element. This is the top level of the cross, which stretches upward toward heaven. It is

never enough that we simply understand the truth of God. We need to come to know this God so that his truth can have its way with us. Humans have to bow to heaven in order to be transformed.

The sermon completes the journey as the preacher looks to *inspire*, the fourth element of integrative preaching. This presses the sermon toward the right extension of the cross, describing the forward movement to a new and better place. Head now unites with heart as the sermon finds its true trajectory.

The movement is centripetal. It pulls the listener inward like the string pulls the stone. It keeps the movement anchored in the center of the cross—engagement to instruction, to conviction, to inspiration. The circle is not closed; rather, it is coiled so that it can be energized.

Coiling the Integrative Model

A coil spring is made of flexible material shaped in the form of a helix. The resulting mechanism can store energy, absorb shock, or maintain a force between two contacting surfaces. The coil produces its energy through centripetal force or torsion.[2] The coil can release that energy in order to achieve a productive result—the kinds of results intended by our preaching.

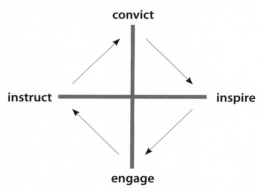

Think about the sermon coiling an integrative tension between these contacting surfaces: human and heaven, head and heart. When that energy is uncoiled, the purposes of the cross are propelled in God's intended direction. This direction is always forward. God is always leading us somewhere different from where we had started. Imagine a coil that stretches upward. The sermon's centripetal motion is always progressive. Our preaching always leads us in a formative direction.

2. M. Wellner, *The Elements of Physics* (New York: Plenum, 1991), 131.

This formational purpose is an intentional act. No one ever preaches by accident. You have to choose to preach.[3] If preaching is going to happen, it is going to be for a purpose. That purpose is the formation of the listener in the image of God and of his will. That the preacher acts by intention is to say that the preacher will undertake specific actions. The preacher will make choices intended for the purpose. This will not be haphazard.

The Material Compounds of Integrative Preaching

This homiletic coil is expressed orally. Its torsion is achieved through the spoken word. Therefore, there are many forms this spoken word can take. The preacher can ask questions, recite poems, make arguments, or give examples. Any of these tactics can help to apply the necessary torque. While the list of these may seem endless, they typically compress to four materials or ways of being in preaching. In keeping with our physical model, these are the *compounds* of the integrative preacher. By application of these materials, the sermon is wrapped around the cross-point and is given its energy and force.

These compounds dwell in the gaps between the crossbeams of the integrative model. They are the result that happens when adjacent elements are compounded. For example, *problems* live between the human and the head at the lower left point of the model, where the mind struggles to appreciate the truth as it is met on the ground. The preacher who is unafraid to speak to problems offers instruction that engages people where they live. Tension is applied to the coil as the sermon gains a sense of authenticity.

A second compound is the *point*, which lives between the head and heaven. This is where the cognitive world of the mind is brought in touch with the objective world of heaven at the upper left quadrant of the model. The point finds its pointedness as it reveals Truth. Instruction then leads to conviction as torque increases on the coil.

The *prayer* is another compound that can be useful to the preacher. Prayer exists at the place where conviction is expressed as inspiration—the upper right-hand segment of the cross. It is the place where the listener's experience of heaven leads to an expression of the heart. Here is where the coil begins to release its force, transforming first the listener and then the world.

A final compound is the *picture*, which finds its physical place in the lower right-hand section of the model. This is the place where inspiration becomes

3. Kenton C. Anderson, *Choosing to Preach: A Comprehensive Introduction to Sermon Options and Structures* (Grand Rapids: Zondervan, 2006), 27.

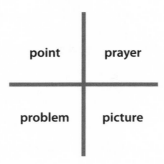

engaging. Through pictures, the preacher offers a vision of the future as it is affected by the message. It is here where the coil extends around to add another layer to its force.

These compounds are the materials that the preacher will use in achieving the elemental functions. It is the picture of the problem that the listener finds engaging. Applying points to problems is the means by which we are instructed. Points that lead to prayer describe the listener's conviction. Prayers that give rise to pictures will inspire our transformation.

Ultimately, transformation happens as we are set in motion. We follow the trajectory of God's intention, and we find we are transformed.

Spiritual Formation through Multiple Coilings

It might take more than just a single sermon. Spiritual formation is a long discipleship—a determined discipline requiring many coilings of the spring. A sermon might go around the circle more than once. Or it might take many preachings of a sustained message till we complete the journey. There might even be some different pathways across the elemental terrain. But in the end, we have been set in motion. We have been formed in Christ by the preaching of the cross. We are in a different place. We will never be the same.

Thinking about formation may encourage us to apply some different terms or ways of being. Spiritual discipline has long been understood as critical to the production of spiritual transformation. As we consider the disciplines that have been found to be productive across the history of the Christian church, we can see how they serve to encourage centripetal force in our model.

We have said that preaching achieves its transformative effect by means of four elemental intentions. Preaching engages by means of problems and pictures. Preaching instructs through making use of points and problems. Preaching convicts through application of points and prayers. Preaching inspires as it utilizes prayers and pictures. It might be helpful to see these functions as summary expressions of the classic spiritual disciplines.[4]

In terms of problems, we might think of the spiritual discipline of guidance. Spiritual direction, counsel, and exhortation have long been understood to be critical ways of encouraging spiritual vitality. To grapple with problems is to express hope of their solution.

Considering points, we might think about the discipline of study, instruction, or meditation. Knowing God well requires understanding him deeply. We will not know him completely until the consummation of his kingdom. But though we might not know him exhaustively, we can know him adequately as he shows himself to us and helps us understand him.

The preacher's tool of prayer well corresponds with a sense of spiritual devotion. Prayer can be expressed more fully through the broader disciplines of fasting, worship, and celebration. As we develop an understanding of God, we are led to a place of communion with God, the very substance of our spiritual discipline.

The picture expresses well the disciplines of service, help, and giving as these are all ways by which our discipline is embodied in the world. Until we can capture our commitment in a disciplined picture of our active response within the world, we have not shown the love required.

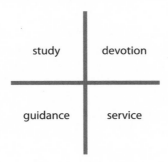

These disciplines can be engaged both personally and corporately in a dual turning of the coil. Believers have long found value in the silence and solitude of a private and personal encounter with God. This first movement might then be personal in nature. Haddon Robinson says that biblical preaching involves the communication of a biblical concept that is applied "first to the preacher" before it is presented to the listeners.[5] Before ever getting to public

4. See, e.g., Richard J. Foster, *Celebration of Discipline: The Path to Spiritual Growth* (New York: Harper & Row, 1978).

5. Haddon W. Robinson, *Biblical Preaching: The Development and Delivery of Expository Messages*, 3rd ed. (Grand Rapids: Baker Academic, 2014), 8.

preaching, the preacher might well begin with preaching to the self, working through the disciplines of guidance, study, devotion, and service.

Our second coiling, then, is corporate in nature. These disciplines are well expressed by means of small group exhortation, corporate proclamation, gathered worship, and public service. The communal expression of these disciplines is amplified in tone and impact as a collective and exponential force is brought to bear.

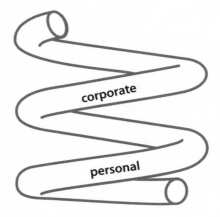

Of course, all of this finds voice in integrative preaching. The preaching of God's Word in the presence of his people by the power of the Spirit offers a means by which these disciplines find their expression.

We have already noticed the integration found in Jesus as described by his disciple John in the opening chapter of his Gospel. Jesus came to offer truth *and* grace, the horizontal axis. He showed himself as Word *become* flesh, the vertical axis. But look to the next verse, John 1:15. John cries out, saying, "He who comes after me has surpassed me because he was before me." Notice the triple coiling of this succinct expression.

John is speaking as a prophet. He is describing what will happen. He is speaking about the one who will come after him. He is talking about how this one who will come after him will surpass him—that any power that his prophetic position might offer will be surpassed and overcome by the one of whom he speaks. This one who will come after will fulfill the promise of the prophecy and achieve the purposes of God.

John says that this one will surpass him because he came before him. The surpassing greatness of the one of whom he speaks is precisely because of his preexistence. In the first verse of this same chapter, John speaks of the Word who was present at creation—who was with God at the beginning. John was a significant figure at the time that he spoke this. He had his own celebrity. But the reason this one who would come after him would surpass him was that he actually came before John. Not in birth order or in genealogical time. The Gospels go to great lengths to establish John as the firstborn and forerunner. This one came first not in calendar time but in cosmic time. This one was born before time and so surpasses all of us.

This promised one was Jesus, the substance of our preaching and the person of the cross. Coil upon coil upon coil—after, before, and above and beyond—we preach the trajectory of Jesus. Word and flesh, grace and truth— the project integrates the purpose of God with the pattern of our preaching.

I have a personal problem with motion sickness. Several surgeries on my left inner ear have made me susceptible to vertigo and instability. I'm not sure

Integrative Preaching Model

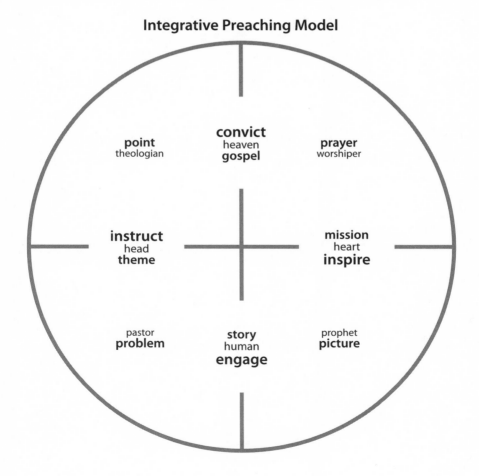

I could handle the Gravitron at this stage in my life. Even thinking about the teacup ride at Disneyland is enough to make me queasy. I do better with rides that have a defined direction. I have found that if I can see where I am going and how the ride will get me there, I have a stomach for it. Remember that motion sickness happens when what our eyes envision is in conflict with what is true inside us. Spiritual illness happens when what we are attracted to conflicts with God's creative purpose for us—when our eyes and our souls do not cohere.

The movement of God will make us well and whole and settled in our stomachs. We need preaching that integrates—preaching that will move us.

PART 2

The Functional Elements of Integrative Preaching

Every sermon must fulfill certain functions if it is to achieve its purpose. You might say that these act as the elemental interests of the integrative sermon.

Classically, we have understood our world to be composed of four primary elements: earth, wind, water, and fire. Of course, any high school chemistry student would see this as oversimplified in contrast to the more precise taxonomy of the periodic table of elements. Nevertheless, there is something to be said for simplicity as we try to work with complex objectives.

Sherlock Holmes is famous for chiding his sidekick with the expression "Elementary, my dear Watson." The suggestion is that problems, when broken down to basic elemental functions, become relatively simple.

Such is true of our preaching. There are ways of speaking that can be considered elemental. Understanding how to utilize these elements will greatly enhance the effect of our preaching. It is easier to act with intention when we have a clear conceptual model of what we are trying to do. The integrative model offers such an elemental approach.

The integrative preaching model is cross-formed, overlaying the horizontal with the vertical, producing four hemispheres, each of which speaks to an elemental aspect of the formational task.

Human—the subjective element
Head—the cognitive element
Heaven—the objective element
Heart—the affective element

As we lay these directions across the X and Y of our homiletic model, we will need to reimagine each as communicative tasks. These, then, will be the four functions that every sermon must accomplish. The absence of any of these will result in an incomplete or *dis*integrated sermon.

Engage—the subjective element (human)
Instruct—the cognitive element (head)
Convict—the objective element (heaven)
Inspire—the affective element (heart)

It might be helpful to think of these as the sermon's *ends*. They are the elemental functions that can be achieved by certain *means*. The means of these functions, then, are as follows:

Story—the means of engagement (human/subjective)
Theme—the means of instruction (head/cognitive)
Gospel—the means of conviction (heaven/objective)
Mission—the means of inspiration (heart/affective)

These four functions, together with their means, comprise the total substance of what our talk is capable of, and the next four chapters will lead us to understand each of them. As we set the model in motion, adjacent elements will integrate, resulting in material compounds that will help the preacher to achieve these elemental effects. Creative communicators will be able to conceive of a vast array of technical approaches, but in the end, all these will come down to the story that engages, the theme that instructs, the gospel that convicts, and the mission that inspires.

5

The Story That Engages

Whenever Jean-Luc Picard, captain of the fictitious starship *Enterprise*, wanted to act on a decision, he would issue a simple, one-word command: *Engage!* By this he declared his intention that the crew of the *Enterprise* would "make it so." It may have been that he wanted to take the ship into warp speed or to launch some form of attack against an enemy. To "engage" meant that the efforts and intentions of the crew would find focus on this singular task whose function would be set in motion. Each crew member was engaged, as was the group that would receive the impact of the command.

To engage an enemy means to demand their full attention. To engage a future spouse means that you are committing fully to this one person, eliminating all the other options. To engage an audience means that your presentation is so compelling that the listeners or viewers cannot be attracted by any other source of input—not unlike the effect of the steely-eyed Picard, whose confidence and command allowed the audience no other option but to give its full attention to *Star Trek: The Next Generation*.

Engage: The Sermon's First Move

The first move of a sermon is to *engage* the audience. This, then, is the first function of the integrative sermon. A sermon cannot be judged effective if it does not engage. Unless it is engaging, it may not even be heard.

A preacher must not assume the listener's attention. Attention is earned. The window by which that attention can be earned is short, and the preacher must be worthy of it. One might well assume that those who have gathered have an interest in hearing what the preacher has to say. After all, they could have chosen to be elsewhere. One might think that the audience, having shown up in church, would want to hear the sermon.

Yet listening is hard. It requires a special kind of energy to resist the pull of other thought streams, especially when the sermon subject is not chosen by the listener. When I sit down to check my social-media feeds, I don't waste time on posts that do not interest me or were not chosen by me. But come Sunday morning I have no choice but to hear what has been offered to me. There is no drop-down menu of options. There is no fast-forward button, except the button in my head that can effectively mute the preacher. You might see me sitting there, and I might look like I am interested. In fact, I might be focused elsewhere—perhaps even on that *Star Trek* rerun that I was watching late last night.

But what about the ones who haven't gathered—that vast throng of humanity arrayed across our communities who have never found themselves in our sanctuaries? If it is hard to hold the attention of those committed to us, what might we have to do to attract the people from the broader harvest? What chance might we have if our preaching is not broadly known to be entertaining? To "entertain" literally means to "hold attention." To hold attention suggests that one might have it to begin with. If our preaching is not engaging, we will never have the opportunity.

So, then, at the very least, our preaching must be engaging. If the audience is not engaged, they will not hear the message that could change their lives. If the listener is not engaged, that person might not come back the next week. People have options, and we might not be thought the best among them.

Tell a Story

The best way to engage listeners is to tell a *story*. Stories are almost irresistible. Storytelling is often disparaged as being for children. Adults are thought to be too sophisticated for this more juvenile form of communication, as if people grow out of the stage whereby story can captivate. But story has no best-before date. Story might be the one form of discourse that is suitable for both the toddler and the PhD.[1] This may, in part, suggest the appeal of

---

1. "Of all the ways we communicate with one another, the story has established itself as the most comfortable, the most versatile—and perhaps the most dangerous. . . . Assembling facts or incidents into tales is the only form of expression and entertainment that most of us

the Bible, whose stories speak powerfully to every intellect and to every level. Story is effective as a means of assuring engagement.

One night a movie came on television just as my wife and I were planning to go to bed. It was not a compelling movie. The reviews were poor, the acting overwrought, the premise questionable. I had already gotten up off the couch to brush my teeth when something about that story caught me. The main character found himself in the hospital, and I could not help but wonder why. Once I knew why the character was in the hospital, I found to my surprise that I needed to know how long he might stay there. I wanted to know what was going to happen to his family while he convalesced—and all this for a fictitious character. I did not particularly care about this character, and he wasn't very well acted. And yet I postponed my bed for several minutes as I engaged the narrative.

If this is the power of a cheaply produced and poorly written rerun movie, what could be the impact of the gospel, told with passion by a present human with a story that could change our life? If you tell the story well and if it is crafted to show its relevance for my life and situation, then I, the listener, like your chances of arresting my daydream. I expect you will engage me.

Pictures and Problems

Story, broadly understood, will be our primary means of encouraging engagement. This is preaching in its subjective sense. It occupies the lower half of the vertical axis, representing the human aspect of the spatial paradigm. It can be expressed in terms of *pictures* (mission) as it leans toward the affective, and of *problems* (theme) when it turns toward the objective. A succinct way of describing story might be that it is "a picture of a problem" or "a problem pictured."

To say that preaching has a subjective element is not to say that it is variable or vagarious. Preaching is driven by its rootedness in the objective Word, and that Word became flesh and dwelt among us. We are speaking about the incarnational nature of preaching. It is a treasured aspect of our theology to appreciate that God was not content to remain distant from his creation. It was because of his love that he took on human flesh and brought himself to us. It is in keeping with the gospel to affirm that God spoke himself into time and space so that we might have the hope of salvation in the person of Christ. If the Son of God could take on flesh, then so can our preaching. The

enjoy equally at age three and age seventy-three." Robert Fulford, *The Triumph of Narrative: Story-Telling in the Age of Mass Culture* (Toronto: Anansi, 1999), x.

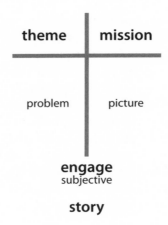

incarnation is the best metaphor for preaching because the Word became flesh. Our preaching ought to do likewise.[2]

An emphasis on engagement appreciates the love that God has for his people. Not content to leave us on our own, God engages us by his Spirit. The preacher who engages audiences by means of story is merely getting into the flow of what God is doing to love his people by his Word.

As engagement leans to the affective side of the model, story is displayed in *pictures*. This is story in the classic "once upon a time" narrative mode, where the presentation unfolds as a series of events. This story can describe real events, or it can be contrived. It can offer an example, or it can set up a tension needing resolution. Whichever way, the story shapes the situation in a manner that the listener can recognize and relate to.

Theological ideas are often offered in the abstract, which can sometimes make them easier to understand. Lifting ideas out of human context can allow for a more dispassionate consideration of complex ideas. This is a useful and important aspect of preaching. But man cannot live by abstractions alone. Unless the sermon is grounded in life, it will not engage distracted people. Sermons need to take the shape of life, unfolding in time just like the listeners do. In this manner listeners will recognize the sermon proposition not merely as logic but as life.

Preachers who know how to engage their listeners understand how to show their propositions as pictures. They don't only know how to describe the truth, but they can see it in their mind's eye, painting the picture for the

2. "Form, methodology, and delivery are nothing more, and nothing less, than the word of God taking on flesh and dwelling among us." Clyde E. Fant, *Preaching for Today*, 2nd ed. (New York: Harper & Row, 1987), xiv.

benefit of the listener. Those who hear are then also able to see the truth as it is shown to them in the form of story.

Engagement can also lean to the cognitive side of the model, taking form as *problems*. Here the story is offered in the nature of a question to be answered or a dilemma that needs to be resolved. This problem can be actual, or it can be hypothetical. Either way, it will engage listeners as they recognize these problems as their own.

Biblical ideas always challenge us because they demand more from us than what we are typically willing to give. Humans are selfish by default. Our primary interest is always our own needs and perspectives. The Bible, then, comes to challenge us toward a broader perspective that looks first to the kingdom and only secondarily to the self. That the biblical perspective is ultimately in our best interest is not always immediately self-evident. We need to be helped to see from that perspective, which is one of the functions of good preaching.

Preaching that engages might then choose to open with this kind of problem. Story, in this sense, is understood broadly as the presentation of a deeply human challenge that the listener relates to because she or he has seen it in life. When the preacher tackles these sorts of problems, listeners will be deeply engaged. We will be compelled to listen to what the preacher is saying because we crave an answer to these challenges. The story of these problems is the story of our lives, and we cannot help but listen to ourselves.

Sometimes preachers shy away from problems in the fear that their preaching might undermine the message that they are trying to establish. But in fact the opposite is true. Listeners struggle with biblical truth innately if not always overtly. These problems are never very far below the surface. Preachers who learn how to surface these problems will find their audience to be more deeply engaged in their preaching.

Engagement, then, can offer either pictures or problems. It can lean in either direction, focusing on cognition or on affection. Sometimes it will even offer both. This is in the inductive nature of preaching. It recognizes that the Bible responds to human need. Rooting the message in the stuff of human life can never fail to be engaging.

How We Tell Our Stories

The story that we tell has several levels. It is in the overlap of stories that our sermon finds its currency. There is of course *his story*, the grand story of salvation that unfolds across time and eternity. This is the story of a God who loved his people so much that he set them free. When in their freedom the people lost their way, this same God made provision for their reconciliation. Completely of grace, this move by God toward his people is the foundation of every story that a preacher would want to tell.

There is also *their story*, the story of the people in the biblical text and to whom the text was written. We never want to forget that the Bible was written into time—real time where people lived and acted out the courses of their lives. Galatia was a real place. The Hittites were real people. And while we are not anxiously pressed by the challenges of Hittite politics, understanding such things can create a surprising common ground and point of connection for our people to our texts.

Certainly there is *our story*, the story of the people to whom the text is focused in its message for today. That starts with the preacher and extends then to the other listeners who follow later in their hearing. The power of the Bible resides in that it is not solely about other people in other times but also about us in our time. God did not just speak in the past. God speaks into the present so that the story of Galatia or of Ephesus is the story of our times and places.

Effective storytelling, then, is found in the overlap between these stories. The best place to preach is where God's story overlaps with their story, such that we come to understand our story. Homiletic storytelling is a Venn diagram with us living out our sermon in the overlapping place.

This is another way of saying that preaching is a living thing. The stories that we tell are not fables. These stories describe the active work of God in the present time to bring out his purposes both past and present. Engagement, then, is more than just being interesting. It is about embracing the work of reconciliation that God is actively achieving through his Word. Preachers are not just spinning yarns or filling time. They are speaking into being the work of God, who is moving in present time to restore his people to relationship with him. To say that preaching must engage, then, is to say that preaching must lead people to engage the God who is reaching them by his Word and by his Spirit.

This is more than mere sermon illustration. It has been common for preachers to understand storytelling as a kind of color commentary, adding vividness to the technical play-by-play. But this underappreciates this theological sense of story.

I remember reading an article many years ago that compelled me by its title: "Raisins in the Oatmeal: The Art of Illustrating Sermons."[3] The article

3. Mark Littleton, "Raisins in the Oatmeal: The Art of Illustrating Sermons," *Leadership* 4, no. 2 (Spring 1983): 63–67.

was helpful, though I will admit that I had difficulty getting past the title. I grew up eating oatmeal every morning for my breakfast. But my mother, understanding that a steady diet of oatmeal can be a little dour, was kind to add a handful of raisins. I love raisins. Sweet and juicy, these raisins made it possible for me to eat the oatmeal. Of course, my mother would never serve me a bowlful of raisins. It was the stick-to-your-ribs qualities of the oatmeal that were thought to provide all the nourishment. The raisins were there simply so that I would consume the nourishing qualities of the oatmeal, which I might otherwise have rejected.

The thought behind the title of this article, then, was that it was the propositional content of the sermon that carried the nutritional weight and not the illustrations. Illustrations were sweet and tasty, and so they were valuable in support of the real spiritual content that was found in the propositions. This betrays a common perception about the spiritual life—that it is almost exclusively, and certainly most significantly, a body of knowledge. The Christian faith is thought to be a set of concepts to be mastered. It is thought to be a catechism more than it is a story to be lived or a relationship to be enjoyed. Preaching, in this spirit, offers spiritually nutritious theological content, which because of its dryness requires something more colorful and appealing to support its digestion. By this model, illustrations are the raisins in the sermonic oatmeal.

This way of thinking would have been news to Jesus, who usually preached in violation of this principle. Jesus's use of story grants you the impression that story was the point and not just the illustration of the point. Of course Jesus offers propositions: "Repent and believe the good news" is about as direct as one can imagine (Mark 1:15). But his preferred method of communication seems to be the parable—stories that work by analogy for those who have "ears to hear" (Mark 4:9). One could argue that the meat of the parable is the underlying propositional meaning, and yet in Jesus's hands the parables seem sufficient in themselves for the purposes that God has in mind. Of course, the parabolic story means nothing without the truth it is meant to convey, but such is the integrative nature of the preaching of Jesus. The unadorned proposition is also insufficient for the purposes of the kingdom as presented by the master teacher.

When fully integrated, stories are the stuff. They do not only suggest the stuff that lies at some deeper and more fundamental level. This is because the story offers the flesh—the human element that breathes life into the word. Some preachers have believed that stories and narrative elements actually obscure the purposes of the sermon and that the way to effectively communicate the truth of an ancient text is to dehumanize the proposition, freeing it from the blood and guts that pollute the pristine nature of the truth.[4] For these preachers, the way to preach an ancient text is to distill a "timeless truth" that can be lifted out of one human context and then transferred into another for reapplication in a different time. While this method does, at least, affirm the applicability of Scripture across time, there is something wrong with a method that is dismissive of the incarnational aspect of God's self-revelation.

The human element is inseparable from the objective point that the Scripture wants to teach. I would argue that retaining the human aspects of the text makes application easier. The task is transposition—re-creating the same biblical theme in a new human time and setting, much like a musician who transposes the same melody and music into a new and different key. Preachers who help listeners see the story in the text are able to help listeners understand their own stories in another place and time.

And there is always a story—in every text there is story, even the book of Romans. You understand that there really were Romans. It is easy to forget by studying Romans that Rome was a city, full of people. The book of Romans is a letter addressed to people in a place and time. If we can grow to understand the Romans (i.e., the first-century people who lived in the city known as Rome) and the fear of separation that they knew, we might grow to understand our own time and place and how it is that we might be encouraged in our troubles to know that nothing can separate us from the love of God in Christ (Rom. 8:39).

There are people in every text. Each biblical pericope was written by a human hand, under the direction of the Holy Spirit, to a particular group of people who needed to hear what God was saying to them in their time. As we grow to understand the human issues of that time, we will better understand what God has in mind for each of us in our time. And that will be engaging.

How we tell our stories, then, will be critical to the effect of the sermon that we preach. The integrative nature of our preaching demands that the stories we tell are driving to a point. If they are not there solely for the purpose of decor, then we need to appreciate what it is that they are doing, and we have to shape our sermons so that they are able to produce the result that we have in mind. This will require a capacity for shaping.

There are many ways to tell a story. You can build a whole world around a story. A listener can get lost within that world if it is too broadly drawn. Sometimes the world of the story is so compelling that the listener wants to

---

4. "In order to principlize without spiritualizing, historicizing, psychologizing, moralizing, or allegorizing, we must first restate the author's propositions *without* including a reference to men or places in our sermon points." Walter C. Kaiser Jr., "The Use of Biblical Narrative in Expository Preaching," *Asbury Seminarian* 34 (July 1979): 14–26.

tell the preacher, "You go on ahead. I'd like to stay here for a while. I will catch up with you later." Sometimes they do not make it back. A story that is told for the sake of the story, and not for the purpose of a God-designed effect, will not be productive.

The preacher needs to know the theme of the sermon. Having understood what the sermon is driving toward, the preacher can then shape the telling of the story for the purposes of delivering that result. It is like driving toward the punch line of a joke. Good comedic practice could be instructive for us on this point. A great stand-up comedian knows how to build a story toward the punch line. Our stories are preparing people for some specific discovery, some particular spiritual payoff. The story is sufficient as a medium, but it is not the end in itself. The story must be carefully shaped so as to achieve the purpose that the preacher has in mind for its telling. Unnecessary details must be discarded. Rabbit trails should be closed. Everything told must be in direct service to the purpose for which the story is intended.

The preacher will want to think, then, about perspective. From which angle should the story be told? Typically, biblical stories are given in sparing detail. The preacher will want to use some imagination to fill in some of the gaps that could bring the story to life. Let's look at an example from the Gospel of Mark.

The Paralytic and His Friends: A Story from Mark 2

In the story of the friends of the paralytic in Mark 2, Mark's telling focuses squarely on the facts: Jesus comes to town and immediately begins preaching. Four men bring a paralytic to hear him, but they cannot get in because of the size of the crowd. So they dig a hole in the roof. That is a compelling story, but only if you use your imagination to seek answers to the obvious questions. Who was this paralytic, and what was it about the man that inspired such determination that these four other men would think it acceptable to do property damage so that they could get their friend to Jesus? Their audacity is breathtaking. How did they get the man up to the roof anyway? That cannot have been easy. Jesus sees this as an act of faith, but how is it that this physical action leads Jesus to take spiritual action, forgiveness of sin? Now we're getting to the nub of the problem—the nature of faith and the courage it requires. If we are to preach this story, we will need to shape the way we tell the story so that it leads directly to the matter of this faith.

It is often not difficult to find an engaging story. In many cases, the story is right there in the text. A set of friends will do anything to bring their friend to Jesus. A group of believers in Rome are about to be driven underground because the emperor needs a scapegoat. A prophet is so overwhelmed by a vision of God's holiness that he volunteers for an impossible mission. A vine is in need of pruning because its unproductive limbs are crippling its growth.

Some of these stories will be more in the nature of a metaphor—a tangible example of something spiritual and necessary. Some will take the nature of a vision—a compelling picture of an imagined future. Others will offer a full narrative arc—a series of events in time that follow after one another to produce an important outcome. In every case, they will set truth in human context. They will engage a listener because he or she will be able to recognize the point of contact for the message in real human life.

The most engaging preachers will learn to tell these stories with a sense of immediacy—not in the past tense but in the present. This is not the telling of dry history, a distant consideration of things long since past. The best storytellers describe their stories not as if they happened (although they might have) but as if they are happening. I remember getting down on my hands and knees to role-play the imagined challenge of getting the paralyzed man up the narrow stairway at the back of the house so as to get up on the roof. I helped the listeners imagine standing inside the house as the bits of dust and clumps of ceiling material began to fall from above, distracting them as they tried to hear Jesus. I helped them hear the thud as the paralytic landed on the floor at Jesus's feet, a little too firmly. Whether any of that actually happened in the exact way that I described, I could not know. I do know that something like these things had to have happened, and so long as my descriptions do not violate the intention of the text, I am helping my listeners by using my imagination to awaken theirs.

It might help us to think like moviemakers. How might we present this story if we were making a film about it? Movies are framed as a series of scenes and shots. The scenes are the locations where the action happens—a room, a street, a field. The shots are the particular angles that the camera uses to focus the viewer's attention. In storytelling, scenes are the venues or settings for whatever is to happen. Shots direct the listener's point of view. Great storytellers drive their agenda by directing the perspective of the listener. This is done by ordering the shots.

The story of the paralytic offers many possible points of view. What is going through the minds of the men as they are lowering their friend through the ceiling? What is their motivation? Can you imagine what is going through the mind of the owner of the house, who is proud to have Jesus visiting but is growing concerned about the possibility of damage to his home? How about the religious leaders at the back of the room? Is that pure disdain on their faces, or is there any hint of faith beginning to stir within their hearts? Shifting the camera angle can be helpful for the listener who might identify more closely with one or the other perspective.

The goal is to engage. This is the functional element that concerns the preacher throughout the sermon, but particularly in its opening stages. Listening to sermons requires a great deal of energy. There are so many distractions. There are too many reasons not to listen. Listeners have things pulling their attention. Does the girl like me? Will I make budget for the fiscal period? Will my team make the playoffs? And what is that black mark on the corner of the ceiling? Is it bigger than it was last week?

Great preachers know how to work with listener distractions, making them work for the preacher instead of against them. If the sermon tells stories that reflect the listener's life experience, or raises problems that reflect the listener's interest, or paints pictures that delight the listener's imagination, there will be engagement. If the listener is engaged, he or she can be led to hear from God.

The preacher asks a lot of the listener. To "engage" might require the courage of a Jean-Luc Picard. Listening to God is not for the faint of heart. The listener is called on to "boldly go" where he or she might have never gone before—into the heart of God and into his will for our life and being.

6

The Theme That Instructs

My family loves board games, especially during holidays such as Christmas when we all have time to spend together. What we are not so good at is following instructions. Our family has a great array of "house rules" that have developed over time and become enshrined among us as the correct way to play the games.

This has proved problematic whenever we welcome others into our game playing. We have noticed, for example, that there are people in the world who take great pains to read and follow the printed instructions that come with a game. When someone appeals to the instructions, our family looks at these printed pages with some mixture of wonder and distaste. The idea that we must adhere strictly to the rules of the game as originally designed seems an unnecessary limitation to us.

This might be a problem for my family. While I may celebrate the independence of our spirit and the creativity we have shown by feeling free to individualize popular board games, this may not be a fitting way to approach matters of greater significance. Instruction matters. The universe contains laws—natural regulations that govern the physical structure of all created things. We will do better by knowing those rules and playing by them.

Playing by ear can bring a certain joy, but improvisation is best practiced by those well instructed in the fundamentals. Listening to a seasoned musician improvise familiar standards can be breathtaking. But artistic license is hard earned, by years of study in the basic rudiments. You earn the right to improvise through a faithful and disciplined attention to the instruction of the masters.

Instruct: The Sermon's Second Move

We have seen that the first move of the integrative sermon is to engage. Having engaged the listeners such that they are attentive to the discourse, the second move is to *instruct*. Instruction is a difficult place to begin a sermon. Most people aren't prepared to dive into deep instruction directly from the beginning, especially people like myself and my family who seem to be disposed to an independence of spirit. It is not that we can't do it. It's just that it is harder to, and it cannot guarantee the result. So the preacher begins with the offer of some kind of story. It may be the picture of a problem (inductive movement), or it may be the problem with a picture (deductive movement), but either way, this story is compelling. It holds the listener's attention.

Now that we know that people are engaged, we are ready to help them learn something—a specific something. We are ready to help people understand the message—the thing that God wants said and understood from Scripture through the Spirit. Great preaching is instructive, but it is a focused form of instruction that we have in mind. The second of the four functions in the integrative model, then, is instruction. The means of this instruction is the theme.

Declare the Theme

Theme, for the purposes of the integrative model, will serve as shorthand for this work of biblical instruction. It will be our designated term for the cognitive work of facilitating an understanding of the Word—the means that encourages the end that is instruction. It is head over against heart, primarily focused on the left side of the horizontal line on the temporal axis. It can be expressed in the subjective as it leans toward story/problem (the problem with the point), or in the objective when it reaches in the direction of gospel/point (the point that speaks to the problem).

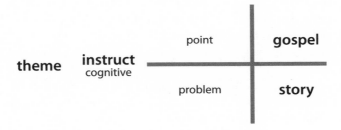

Instruction acknowledges the central importance of the intellect in human transformation. Romans 12:2 says that we are transformed by the renewing of our minds. While it is not enough to simply think correctly, we will never live well until we think well.

Problems and Points

As instruction works in the direction of story, it takes an inductive shape. Instruction that responds to the subjective concern of the listener will focus as the "problem with the point."

Human listeners will always have *problems* with a biblical theme. Like my problem with board games, we have a problem taking instruction. We want to follow our own direction—to design our own instruction. Given our inherent limitations, this is not our best option. The limitations imposed by space and time cripple our capacity to form our own fundamentals with any kind of long-term effectiveness. Imprisoned by the restrictions of our personal perspective, we simply do not see far enough or well enough to chart a reliable path for ourselves. There is just too much we do not know and cannot ever know.

The fundamental human problem is this chronic state of independence. We live in a constant, default state of rebellion against the way of God. We simply think we know better and that we can do better by our own instruction. We live with this tremendous state of unwarranted personal confidence that tells us that we can do no better than the wisdom we can conjure by our own imagination. This approach would be absolute folly if applied to medicine or law or air traffic control, but it defines the fundamental arrogance of the natural human state. Pride is the very definition of sin.

Whenever we seek to press a biblical theme on the world, there will be trouble. People struggle in this world. We try to understand why our marriage disappoints us or why we cannot trust our colleagues. We are frustrated by the fact that sometimes lying pays better than telling the truth and that fear offers better protection than love. There are always problems.

The theme speaks to such problems. We will not always remove trouble by our talking, but we can point to truth that can solve the riddle of our futility. When we are hurting, the application of the Word is a salve that offers healing and encouragement. When the theme we teach is seen to resolve trouble, it will be appreciated.

Theme can also lean in the direction of the gospel, and as it does, it acts as deduction. It will make plain a *point*. Instruction that respects the givenness of truth will put that point to the problem.

People have largely given up on truth, at least as it touches on the biggest questions of our life, identity, and way of being. Truth seems beyond us—certainly beyond our capacity to preach. Even if we could understand what is true for our personal existence, the thought that we could know truth for others well enough to proclaim it to a gathered group seems to be the acknowledged limit of our arrogance. We might have some level of confidence about our own selves, at least until things break down, but we have little hope of identifying truth for others. Even when we do think we have some proven insight to offer, it will likely not be well received if pressed with a tone of too much confidence.

Yet preachers have that kind of confidence, not because of our own personal wisdom, but because we believe that God has spoken and is speaking through his Word and by his Spirit. As we fall into the stream of what God is saying, we actually believe that there is truth that we can know and truth that we can share. We preach because we know that God is speaking—not solely that he spoke but also that he speaks. God has not left us without witness in the world. Theologically, commitment to instruction displays our embrace of God's work of self-revelation. God is making himself known in the world, in part through preachers who instruct people in his Word.[1]

Preaching seeks to bring this truth to bear on the problems that engage us. This is the substance of our preachers' instruction—an integrated point and problem, expressed in the form of a coherent theme. One could say that the theme *completes* the story, like a caption to a cartoon or the lyrics to the music.

How We Declare Our Themes

The sermon theme is a collection of words focused on a particular intention and shaped to be retained. It is the sermon in summary, the "big idea" that forms the payoff for the listener's engaged investment. It is the substance of the preacher's instruction.

While we have seen that engagement is the first move of the sermon, it might not be the first move in our assembly of the sermon. It might be helpful to start by working on instruction. Until we know the sermon's theme, it will be difficult for us to understand our manner of engagement.

1. "God speaks. God's self-revelation includes words which are intended to communicate. The ability to communicate in words is an aspect of our creation in God's image." Peter Adam, *Speaking God's Words: A Practical Theology of Expository Preaching* (Downers Grove, IL: InterVarsity, 1996), 55.

The theme is the center pole of the integrative sermon. First and foremost, we are going to establish the sermon's big idea. A big idea or theme is a concise expression of the message being taught.[2] The theme summarizes the intention of the biblical text for a particular audience in a specific moment in time. When we get the theme right, everything else finds its place. Without clarity about our intention, our talk will flounder. Without focus, we will have a hard time sustaining interest.

Any biblical text will propose several ideas, some of which are big enough to preach. It can feel like we are cheating the text when we try to distill a single proposition for the purposes of communication. Yet this underappreciates the unity of the biblical text. At its core, the Bible offers one big idea—the reconciliation of the creation to its Creator, from which every sermonic idea finds its center and its source.

So how do we discern which idea to preach? We read the text, and we derive our idea from a faithful exegesis. The idea that we settle on might not be the largest idea that the text has to offer. There are big ideas and bigger ideas, but the one we settle on will be big enough to preach. We listen to the text, and we listen to the Spirit in the context of the community, and we discern what God wants us to say. If we find it in the text of Scripture, it will be sufficient for our preaching, provided that we can locate the truth within the lived experience of our people.

The Word of God is speaking in the present tense. To be truthful, I am not terribly interested in the Philippians. What I mean is that I do not live in Philippi and I do not know any Philippians. I live in Vancouver, and so my primary interest is in Vancouverites because those are the people whom I preach to. I appreciate that if I intend to get Vancouver right, I am going to have to get Philippi right, because that is the means by which I hear the voice of God. God spoke through Paul to the Philippians in part so that I can hear his voice for the Vancouverites. The Philippians knew nothing about twenty-first-century Vancouver. That the text spoke every bit as powerfully to them does not diminish the present tense power of the Word as heard today. God is making himself known in the world through his Word, and as he speaks, we ought to pay attention to his instruction.

Getting the theme right depends on a careful reading of the biblical text. This cannot be overstated. Far too often we come to the Bible with a preconceived notion of what it says and what it means. But to determine our

2. "Terminology may vary—central idea, proposition, theme, thesis statement, main thought—but the concept is the same: an effective speech 'centers on one specific thing, a central idea.'" Haddon W. Robinson, *Biblical Preaching: The Development and Delivery of Expository Messages*, 3rd ed. (Grand Rapids: Baker Academic, 2014), 17.

theme faithfully we have to come to the text with a desire to hear it fresh. This means that we are actually going to have to read it. As we read and as we analyze, the question will be twofold. We want to know what the text is talking about (the subject) and what it is saying about what it is talking about (the complement).[3]

For example, a subject might be "the love of God." That is a fine subject for discussion, but as a theme it leaves the preacher wanting. There is nothing here to proclaim. To say we speak about the love of God is to only narrow the field. We have not yet said whether we appreciate God's love. We have said little about its nature. There is nothing yet that can be affirmed or denied or fought over. A subject without a complement has no point and speaks to no problem.

We need to add a complement to our subjects to complete our expressions so that they become full proclamatory statements. We could say, for example from 1 Corinthians 13:8, that the love of God is never failing. The subject (what the text is talking about) is God's love. The complement, then (what the text is saying about what it is talking about), is that it never fails. Now we have something that we can get angry over or give our life for. Now we have something to proclaim.

This is an effective way of testing the quality of one's theme: Does the theme offer us anything that we could argue over? I could tell you that the subject of our conversation is concussions in NFL football. As a subject, you may or may not find that interesting, but as a subject without a complement, there is nothing contentious under consideration. If I told you, however, that NFL football should be banned because of the risk of catastrophic injury and an attendant sense of barbarism, now we have something that could cause an argument. Now we have a subject plus a complement.

I could tell you that the subject of our sermon is Christ's atonement. So far, so good. I may have piqued your interest, but I have not yet picked a fight. If I tell you that the atonement of Christ is the vicarious, substitutionary appeasement of God's wrath, we have something that could produce an argument. This is not to say that preaching must always be controversial or that it must always lead to fighting. It is to say that preaching must always go on record. It must always stake a claim. If we do a good job of making our case, we may avoid the argument, but the argument must always be risked. If we are going to preach the Bible, then that risk is always going to be real. If we are proclaiming something, we just might get in trouble. If we have played it safe, by introducing subjects without complements, we really haven't preached.

3. Ibid., 21–22.

The intention of our instruction is this proclamation. Preaching needs to contend for something. Until there is something proclaimed—something in contention—we really haven't preached.

It is in this establishment of a proclaiming theme that we bring a heaven-formed theology to our human problems while grounding our theology in the pastoral challenges of human life.

The theme, of course, is just the sermon in a nutshell. It is what makes the sermon portable, offering a concise and memorable expression of the fuller piece. It is a succinct expression of everything the sermon wants to say. When offered well, it is the thing that nags the listener long after the sermon has concluded.

That means that the sermon will offer a much fuller instruction of the sermon's shorthand. The theme will not be made solely on the strength of its aphoristic appeal. The success of the theme will depend on its underlying argument.

This is where the problem can occur. Not all presentations are instructive. Not all themes will be persuasive. Ideas can be unconvincing. Sometimes they are muddled by confusing logic, unreasonable warrants, irrelevant facts, or disreputable endorsements. The presence of any of these will discredit the proposition entirely.

A great theme will clarify rather than obscure, through careful definition, appropriate division of thought, the quantification of reality, and compelling restatement. Great thematic preaching will critique, seeking to approve, disprove, and improve the propositions offered elsewhere. An effective theme helps us to think with the mind of God.

Confusion happens when instruction is poorly ordered or improperly defined. We need to start with a common vocabulary. This means that we must define our terms. We can disagree on what a word means, but we will not be able to talk with each other until we are all agreed as to what we mean by what we say. Using jargon is an act of arrogance. It adds exclusion to confusion. So we should not use it unless the technical term is helpful in clarifying truth.

It may be that the term *atonement* is necessary to our presentation. If so, we will want to use our definition of the term as an opportunity to invite people into a deeper and more profound appreciation for our truth. We do not throw up theological terms as a means of vetting listeners, like the bar that indicates how tall you need to be to ride the roller coaster. This is not a prideful way of gathering the select and special ones. We might, however, use an unfamiliar term as a way of distinguishing an idea that can be seen as special. Through careful and winsome definition, we can see people delight in discovery of something they had not previously understood.

Our preaching can also be confusing when things are out of order. People need to understand how one idea leads to the next as the logical consequence of a concept already established. We need to be careful not to move too quickly so that people can see how things follow. We might want to consider shorter intervals between ideas so that the gaps are not too large.

I could tell you, for example, that a lot of preaching is uninspiring. That is an idea that corresponds to a lot of people's experience. I could then say that uninspiring preaching is the cause of church decline. A lot of listeners might readily agree, but for others it might not follow that the one thing leads naturally to the other. There could be a lot of reasons for the decline of the church. It may not even be a given that the church is in fact declining. We may need a few more warrants to prove our claim.

First we would need to define what we mean by uninspiring preaching. Then we would need to define how we might recognize a church that is in decline. From there we would want to establish a connection between the preaching that happens and how it affects the vitality of the church. These things cannot be assumed if we wish our argument to be convincing.

There is a danger that, in tracing the lineage of our argument, we could strip the life right out of it. This is where the art comes in. A great communicator will lead the listener through the logic in a way that is delightful and not doleful. For example, if we have concern about church decline, it can bring joy to discover that better preaching might make a difference.

Sometimes we have to differentiate one thing from another. Identifying and separating the component parts of a text, a proposition, or an argument can be helpful in terms of seeing how these things work and how we might assign relative value to the various parts. This is where grammatical analysis is helpful as we try to distinguish this *and* this as opposed to this *or* this. It makes a difference that Jesus offered grace and truth, not grace as opposed to truth, and it matters that we know the difference.

Once people understand what we are saying, we can move to encourage adoption of our claims. We need to help people understand why our proposition is important, showing why and how it can be valued. It might be helpful to name the stakes involved in acceptance or rejection. Preachers ask a lot of listeners. We cannot presume the listener will respond just because the message has been made clear.

Sometimes what we need is reinforcement. It may be that the theme we speak will be a word already known and appreciated. The goal then will be to deepen the impact of the familiar word through repetition, restatement, and perhaps even renovation of the underpinnings for the claim.

Great preaching offers warrants that can bear the weight our themes demand. Our instruction must make sense to people. When it does, we may find that people are convinced. To summarize, the underlying argument of a sermon's theme includes the following steps:

- define the terms
- order the arguments
- differentiate the components
- reinforce the claims

The Word That Must Be Spoken

In the beginning was the Word.

At the core of all being is the Word. This is to say that existence is founded on a concept. To say that something is conceptual is to say that it has meaning—that there is something to it that can be analyzed and understood. If a thing can be understood, it will have purpose and can take shape as the substance of instruction. To say that the Word was the conception point of the universe, the trigger that incited all existence, is to say that the universe has purpose and meaning and that its purpose and meaning can be communicated.

A Word must be spoken. The Greek word *logos*, meaning "word" or "reason," is rooted in the cognate word *lego*, meaning "to speak." To speak requires content, hence the necessity of words. The foundational conception of the universe is that it is to be spoken, that its truth is to be instructed such that it can be known. Knowing truth is a process of logical thought—the definition, analysis, and ultimate communication of meaning-bearing words, such as is being practiced here. It is often thought to be a sterile exercise, best practiced with scientific precision in pristine environments.

Except that this Word is capitalized. When the apostle John began his Gospel, his Word was a person. "In the beginning was the Word, and the Word was with God, and the Word was God. He was with God in the beginning" (John 1:1–2). The expression of the gospel is that the core of existence is not so much a concept but a person—the person of Jesus Christ. To know the universe and its meaning is to know Jesus, and Jesus can be known because he was a preacher—Jesus is the Word. This Word must be shared. We must be instructed in this Word such that we come to know and understand it—that we might truly know the God who is making himself known through his Word.

Instruction in the Word is an elemental aspect of integrative preaching. It is not an affront to our personal creativity or to our independent spirit.

Transformation happens by the renewing of the mind (Rom. 12:2). Preaching simply isn't preaching unless people have learned something. If our listeners do not go away with deepened ways of thinking, the sermon has failed. We ought to celebrate the opportunity. God has not left us in the darkness. He speaks so we might know. Preachers do not shrink from this shining of the light, this instruction in the Word.

7

The Gospel That Convicts

Galileo Galilei is often described as the father of modern physics for his groundbreaking work in the natural sciences. Fascinated by natural phenomena such as tides and pendulums, he was compelled to hold some unpopular convictions, notably heliocentrism, the idea that the earth revolved around the sun and not the other way around.

This idea is self-evident today, but try to imagine what it would have been like to hold such an idea in the early seventeenth century. Geocentrism held that the earth occupied the central place within the universe. This was taken to be a matter of biblical fidelity. Psalm 104:5 says that God "set the earth on its foundations; it can never be moved." Ecclesiastes 1:5 says that "the sun rises and the sun sets, and hurries back to where it rises." Our current hermeneutical values help us to appreciate texts such as these for their contextual intention, but it is not hard to see how a literal reading of such texts might have put a man like Galileo offside.

Galileo's conviction cost him his freedom. Brought before a papal inquisition, he was found guilty of encouraging heresy and was sentenced to imprisonment, later commuted to house arrest, under which he was incarcerated for the rest of his life. His intellectual conviction led to a judicial conviction, such that Galileo experienced both meanings of the term.

Preachers need to be careful. Ideas have consequences, and ideas expressed publicly can have serious effects. Preachers are accountable for what they say. They had better have conviction about the things they preach, for they will answer for those things in the court of opinion as well as in the courts of the land.

Convict: The Sermon's Third Move

Conviction is not to be feared. Conviction is one of the four functional elements of the integrative sermon. The sermon must engage the listener. The sermon must instruct the listener. But the sermon must also convict, or it cannot well be called a sermon.

Certainly the preacher must bring his or her own conviction. In 2 Timothy 3, Paul establishes two forms of authority for the message he is preaching. There is the primary authority of the Scripture itself, which is breathed by God and is therefore profitable for teaching, reproof, and correction (vv. 16–17). But there is also the authority offered by the preacher's own life and experience. "You have known my teaching," Paul says, "my way of life, the persecutions and sufferings I endured, the places I have been" (see vv. 10–11). In other words, Paul offers his own experience—his personal conviction—as evidence of the authority of his message. Truth is truth, even if the preacher does not believe it, but when the preacher embodies conviction, the message is infused with an enhanced authority.

People are especially hungry for conviction in these postmodern times. The fundamental feature of postmodernity is uncertainty. The one thing we know is how much we do not know. The more we know about what we do not know, the less confident we become about any of it. People are easily moved because there seems to be nothing firm or permanent on which one can gain a foothold. We used to think the sun revolved around the earth. One day we might find the things we understand today are just as insecure. Conviction is in short supply.

When we find it, conviction is contagious. When people bring conviction, it tends to pass along to others. People who lack conviction are attracted to those who have it, precisely because of its rarity. When it's discovered, however, it replicates and multiplies. It never exhausts itself. People looking for conviction find it in others, and rather than taking it from them, they find themselves able to generate their own from the seed offered by the other. They are able to share that conviction with even more others yet, such that the effect builds on itself.

Good preachers have conviction, but it is the development of conviction in the listener that marks the sermon as effective. The objective of the sermon is to see the listener transformed. Lasting transformation will not happen until the listener has developed conviction about the sermon theme. This is conviction in both senses of the word. Conviction describes a depth of commitment to a concept or a direction. But there is also the judicial sense of the term, as Galileo found out. Preaching entails both senses of the word.

Preaching happens in the presence of God. "In the presence of God and of Christ Jesus . . . I give you this charge: Preach the word" (2 Tim. 4:1–2). The authority of God stands over us and holds us accountable for the things we do, the things we are, and the things we say. To stand before God is to be convicted by him. "Woe to me. . . . I am ruined," says Isaiah when he finds himself stripped bare before the presence of the holy God (Isa. 6:5).

This conviction is quite literal. We stand as preachers in the presence of God, "who will judge the living and the dead" (2 Tim. 4:1). If we are found unworthy, we will be convicted in the most literal sense. We will face judgment and conviction, resulting in eternal death. This is our reality absent the offer of grace and gospel, which is what empowers the preaching that we bring.

Present the Gospel

Our means of conviction is the *gospel*. Just as the means of engagement is story and the means of instruction is theme, the means by which we manage this conviction is the gospel—the good news of grace that makes possible our standing before the face of God.

First John 4:17 reminds us that the love of God has been made perfect in us, such that we can stand in confidence before God on the day he judges us. There could be no more fearful prospect than to stand in the presence of the one who has all authority and who knows everything about us, and who is absolutely jealous for righteousness. But, according to verse 18, perfect love drives out fear—even this fear, the fear of ultimate, eternal conviction and condemnation. Yet God in his fundamental character defines this very love. He is love, ontologically, in the depth of his very being (vv. 7–8). In his deep, abiding love, God sent his Son, Jesus, to be the propitiation, or satisfaction, for our sin. This was the defining act of love that has forever established the possibility of love between people and toward the God who first loved us.

Imagine standing before a judge. You are guilty, and you know it. Everyone in the courtroom knows it, including the judge who declares your conviction. But then, before this conviction can be enacted, the judge points out his son, who is sitting in the courtroom. He loves his son more than he loves himself. He also loves you, and out of that love he calls forward his son, this man who has had nothing to do with your crime. He asks his son to bear the judgment of your sentence, and this son willingly and graciously consents to do so. You now are free. You are altered, but you are free.

This is the gospel. We can stand before the presence of God. We hear his Word and embrace it with conviction, but not because our personal strength, credentials, or righteousness has made us immune. We stand because we have been forgiven as an act of grace by the very God who stands in judgment over us. Without grace, conviction would imprison us and leave us hopeless. But given grace, we can stand with conviction and serve the living God.

Gospel is the means by which the preacher drives conviction. This is preaching in its objective sense. It occupies the upper half of the vertical axis, representing the heaven aspect of the center (spatial) line. It can be expressed in terms of points (theme) as it leans toward the cognitive, or it can be expressed in terms of prayers (mission) as it bends in the direction of the affective. The gospel is the "point turned to prayer" or the "prayer that rises from the point."

To say that gospel is an objective element is to say that it is the full and final expression of reality. The gospel is the most congruent description of the relation of the sovereign God to his creation. There is nothing more fundamental, nothing more significant, nothing more that could be said but that God has acted to reconcile the world to himself through the cross.

To preach the gospel is to preach like Jesus, whose very life and being embodied this preaching of the cross. After John was arrested, Jesus came preaching, "proclaiming the good news of God. 'The time has come,' he said. 'The kingdom of God has come near. Repent and believe the good news!'" (Mark 1:14–15). Jesus's life, death, and message found their focus on the gospel from the beginning of his ministry. Preaching that offers the gospel continues in the spirit of Jesus's own preaching.

Points and Prayers

As conviction leans in a cognitive direction, it responds in terms of *points*. This describes how the gospel takes its shape as belief. Having been instructed in the truth, the listener is now led to affirm those beliefs and to be convinced of them.

It is sometimes thought that clarity of explanation is sufficient for preaching. If we have made ourselves clear, we think we have done our job. "I have made my point," the preacher is often satisfied to say. But simply leading someone to understand the truth is not the end goal of preaching. Even the demons understand the truth (James 2:19). The challenge for preaching is to lead people from understanding to faith—from instruction to conviction. Preaching for conviction involves instruction but goes beyond it to lead people to appreciate, affirm, and ultimately give their lives to the point of the gospel.

Conviction, then, is more than just a feeling of confidence. Conviction is founded on truth, carefully instructed and deeply understood. It rises from a sense that not only is this true, but it is true for me. And if it is true for me, it can be true for the world.

As conviction moves toward an affective direction, it finds its form as *prayer*. This is where the ideational conviction becomes relational. Having understood the truth of God, we now find ourselves exposed before the person of God.

Conviction must express itself in words of repentance, words of gratitude, and words of praise. As we stand before his holy presence, reconciled by his grace, there are things that we must say. Preaching is an oral medium. It must be spoken. We will need to say sorry to God, to say thank you to God, to say, "Lead me, O God."

This is where the sermon moves from head to heart. Preaching must always be more than just an understanding of God. It must also be an experience of God.[1] This is where gospel conviction becomes personal.

This will be the sermon's "big moment." We understand the sermon needs to have a "big idea," but it also needs a big moment, a climax in God's presence toward which the sermon builds. Sermons are like songs. They need to crescendo. They need to grow and build to a particular moment when all of a sudden it all makes sense. Everything falls into place in this holy moment because we finally understand that we have heard from God.

This kind of moment is a lot to aspire to, but preaching will not achieve its full potential until it comes to a climax. It does not need to be forced. The

---

1. "The central purpose of preaching is the disclosure of God, an encounter with God through the Word, more than information about God." Paul Scott Wilson, *The Practice of Preaching* (Nashville: Abingdon, 1995), 20.

preacher does not have to contrive conviction. The preacher only needs to be conscious about staying at the task until instruction has had its full effect. We will not stop with teaching. We have to keep going, courageously pushing on until the sermon finds us at the foot of the cross. The Holy Spirit will do the heavy lifting if we don't give up too quickly. It we can stay in the moment, we will hear from God. We will understand his presence. We will have to take our shoes off because we understand that we are on holy ground.

I remember preaching at an unfamiliar church in Seoul, South Korea. As the pastor guided me to the platform, he led me to stop and remove my shoes. As we ascended the pulpit area, I was compelled to stand on a pillow as I offered the sermon. I am not certain as to all of the cultural considerations involved in preaching while standing on a pillow. Perhaps the pillow was there because the regular preacher had some kind of ailment in his feet. Perhaps it was to provide some small elevation in height. Perhaps I misunderstood the situation completely. All I know for sure is that while I stood there, my feet on that pillow, I was led to a renewed awareness that this was holy ground. I was speaking for God. I was his unworthy mouthpiece, and the only reason I could stand there at all was because of the gospel that I preached. I do not know whether I was able to lead the people to that same recognition. Linguistic and cultural barriers made that hard to tell. I only know that I had my own moment in the presence of God as point became prayer under conviction by the gospel.

How We Offer the Gospel

I want to offer the gospel every time I preach. If we miss this moment, our application will be merely moralistic. Moralism is preaching that calls us to be better people—to be better Christians who pray more, read the Bible more, and do more tasks because it is right and good. These are worthy aspirations, but they will not be sustainable if we have never met with God. Morality is a poor substitute for the gospel. Moral suasion requires us to be strong enough and resolved enough to be whatever we believe we need to be. We might be able to carry it off for a little while, but in the end we will fail because that is what human beings do. Even young people grow tired and weary (Isa. 40:30). We all have our limits. We can only be so moral for so long. We will all fall short of the glory of God (Rom. 3:23).

This is why we need the gospel. We need an objective solution, a resource that is above and beyond the weakness of our personal limitation. Humans can run fast, but only so fast. Someone might shave a tenth of a second off the world-record 100-meter time at the next Olympics, but they will not shave off seconds. It is safe to say than no one will ever run 100 meters in five seconds. No one will ever swim across the Atlantic Ocean. No human will ever broad jump the Mississippi River. We can do better, but we will never do everything that we can hope for or imagine, except that God should intervene.

The gospel could have only come from heaven. It is objective in the sense that it is the heaven-constructed solution for all humankind. It is like discovering an alien metal or an otherworldly element. The gospel could not have been conceived or created by humans because it is the product of heaven. Whenever we come to see this, we are gobsmacked. Encountering gospel conviction is always a stop-in-your-tracks, smack-in-the-face kind of moment that arrests us, enthuses us, and redirects us in the way that we should go. It is the biggest of moments. If we miss it, we are doomed to the merest moralism.

Developing this moment might seem artificial if we understand it to be contrived by the preacher's choices and intentions. It might seem unwelcome if it becomes a predictable preacher move—wait for it, here it comes, there it is. World-weary preachers might try to manipulate congregations to this kind of moment, like the evangelistic preacher who dims the lights, cues the organ, and asks for just as many verses of "Just As I Am" as he feels is necessary to achieve the result he feels will validate him. Preaching for these people is a mechanical exercise, designed to achieve a programmed result, as if by turning a crank. Preaching under this conception is a mathematical formula: content + cadence + conviction = contentment, compensation, and not a little cynicism.

But this does not mean that we cannot come to preaching with a sense of holy expectation.[2] Stanley Grenz writes that prayer is "laying hold of God's willingness."[3] He means that seeking the things that God already promised is not about trying to convince God to do something that he is likely to withhold. God is not grudging with his blessing. He has declared his desire to be heard by us, and as we are intentional about opening the opportunity to engage God, we can be confident that he will not leave us at the altar. God will meet us. The bush will burn.

---

2. "How can we handle dynamite and not expect it to explode." Haddon Robinson, "Holy Expectation," in *The Art and Craft of Biblical Preaching: A Comprehensive Resource for Today's Communicators*, ed. Haddon Robinson and Craig Brian Larson (Grand Rapids: Zondervan, 2005), 112–13.

3. "This means that when we pray we lay hold of and release God's willingness and ability to act in the world he has created." Stanley J. Grenz, "The Amen Rebellion," *Christianity Today*, October 7, 1991, 24.

We come to conviction in the same manner that we come to worship. We understand that God loves to be worshiped by us. He longs to meet with us and to bless us with his presence. We do not have to apologize for seeking God's presence. We show up. We open our mouth and express our conviction. So God shows up, and together we see what he intends to do.

This is where God in the person of the Holy Spirit becomes especially evident. We cannot predict how the Spirit will affect us. We cannot predict which way the wind will blow. We only know that it will blow, and so we place ourselves within its stream and let it fill our sails. We allow ourselves to be directed by the Spirit, and we anticipate the result.

Anticipation is a major skill for the preacher. When Wayne Gretzky played hockey, it was said that his primary asset was his ability to anticipate the play. He was not the strongest skater, the biggest hitter, or the sharpest shooter. But what he could do better than anyone else was anticipate. He knew where the puck was going before anyone else, and that is where he would go.

Preachers anticipate that God is going to act. Great preachers have a knack to get to where God is going and to meet him in the work he is doing. Preaching, then, is not about inventing things for God to do. It is about appreciating what he has already declared himself to be doing and to meet him there. This kind of anticipation is spiritually discerned. It comes from hours in prayer and in the Word. It comes from walking with God and learning his ways across long spans of time. This is why preaching is trusted sparingly to novices. The best preachers will not live off youthful enthusiasm. Great preachers will build out of a long practice in the same direction.[4] Knowing God, they lead others in the way of God.

Clearing Space for the Spirit

While we cannot dictate to the Spirit, we are going to have to clear space for the Spirit. We cannot load our sermons so full of material that we have no time to actually hear from God, which is what the whole exercise is supposed to be about. We need some white space in our sermons, some spatial clearings wherein God can do his thing.

Conviction needs sermonic time and space. We have to plan for this, or we will rush right past it. This does not mean long periods of silence, though that might not always go awry. It does mean that we might have to slow our flow. It might mean we learn the value of a pregnant pause. Perhaps it will

4. Eugene H. Peterson, *A Long Obedience in the Same Direction: Discipleship in an Instant Society* (Downers Grove, IL: InterVarsity, 2000).

require more repetition, a different cadence, and a different form of physical presentation. Perhaps we will need to look up more. Perhaps we will need to get out from behind the pulpit or the podium. We are going to need to do something tangible—something physical—to indicate that we are clearing room for something different to happen.

It might mean that we literally adopt the postures and vocabulary of prayer. Prayer does not just have a place as an addendum to the sermon. It needs to be the framework of the entire sermon—and certainly at this moment of conviction. If we need to thank God or to say sorry to God, we had best do it audibly and purposefully, and we had better make sure that there is time for it.

Father, forgive us, we have known so little what we do. Forgive us for the pride and arrogance of our preaching. Forgive us for rushing too quickly past your presence. Forgive us for those times we have thought we have known better than you, adopting our own conceptions because we have been too afraid to embrace your convictions. Thank you, Lord, for gifting us sufficiently that we can speak on your behalf. We do not count ourselves worthy of this privilege, but we are grateful.

Most of all, Lord, help us to be effective for the benefit of our listeners and to the praise of your glory. We know this is not for our glory but for yours. Forgive us every time we mix that up. And as we continue in this process of reflection on our calling as preachers, may you inspire something better in us, some deepening of our conviction and our sense of calling. You have loved us on the cross, and you have gifted us in Christ. This we will preach. This, we trust, you will bless.

(Long pause.) I trust you found that wasn't out of place. Instruction ought to lead to conviction. These are elemental functions. Preaching will not be great in the absence of either.

Galileo, as an example of conviction, was not perfect. He felt the tension of wanting to be faithful to his God while trying to follow where the science led him. He buckled under pressure, attempting to find ways while under oath to deny his guilt while sustaining his science. Under inquisition, he tried to deny what he had written, seeking to squirm from the consequence that his conviction required. The man was human. Yet the reason we are still talking about him today is that in the end he was unable to deny what he knew to be true. According to popular legend, after recanting his theory that the earth rotated around the sun, he allegedly muttered under his breath, "And yet it moves."

And the earth does move, around and around and around again. The world is constantly in motion, according to the laws that God himself has established. But its movement has a purpose—it has trajectory.

It is that motion that the preacher serves—leading people in the direction of the gospel, to an encounter with the holy God himself. As we meet him, we will know him, and we will be known by him.

8

The Mission That Inspires

Forty years before Copernicus and Galileo, Leonardo da Vinci proclaimed that the "sun does not move." Two hundred years before Isaac Newton, Leonardo proposed the law of gravity. How was it possible for this man to offer some of the most cogent and far-reaching scientific conclusions ever described, while at the same time producing some of the most beloved and compelling works of art the world has ever seen? *The Last Supper* was no small achievement. The *Mona Lisa* continues to inspire.

It is tempting to think that Leonardo was abnormally gifted and that his genius was simply born to him. No doubt, there was a special gifting to this man. That gift was his curiosity. Leonardo had an insatiable appetite for knowledge and a particular bent toward integration. Art was science and science art.[1] *Vitruvian Man* was as much about mathematics and physics as it was about beauty and anatomy. The beauty of the world could not be observed without an accompanying focus on its underlying structure. Mathematical formula could not find utility until it was seen in the flesh.

It was Leonardo's curiosity that led him to these inspiring integrations. The better he understood something, the more it motivated him. The more motivated he found himself, the better able he was to express his findings through his art. Leonardo's notebooks were probably his greatest form of art, not solely in the drawings but in the ideas that he conceived. Leonardo thought about motion, about the natural environment, about flying machines,

1. Martin Clayton, *Leonardo da Vinci: The Anatomy of Man* (Boston: Little, Brown, 1992), 15.

and about bemused women. In every case, the art derived from the science as the science was inspired by the art. The result was a body of work that continues to inspire—to move people to more enlightened ways of being.

Inspire: The Sermon's Final Move

The fourth and final functional element of integrative preaching is *inspiration*. A great sermon will result in something. It cannot sit idle; it must propel things into the future. A good sermon will engage its listeners. It will instruct its listeners. It will lead its listeners to conviction. But until the sermon inspires its listeners, it will be incomplete.

Inspiration derives from the same root as *respiration*. It is about breath. To say that we are inspired is to say we have been inflated, filled full of life-expanding air. Inspired people are alive. They are breathing. Living people are in motion. They are engaged, which completes for us the integrative circle.

One doesn't need breath to sit motionless. A deflated balloon will not elevate. An airless ball will never bounce. Respiration is required for health and mobility. A sermon that is not filled with breath will not live or move or have its being (Acts 17:28).

We describe the Bible as having been inspired by God. Second Timothy 3:16 says that "all Scripture is God-breathed," which is a more literal way of speaking of its inspiration. To say that the text has been breathed by God is to say that it comes from inside him. It says that the words of Scripture describe the very life of God. The Bible speaks the will, the way, and the nature of God. It is not merely about God. It does not even only speak for God. It is the breath of God, which means that it is inseparable from him.

This is a lot to make of this one metaphor, but consider the alternative. To be without breath is to be without life. If Scripture is not breathed by God, then it does not carry the power of God. Without inspiration, it is just another book—a good book, perhaps, but not adequately transformative.

To say, however, that a sermon must offer inspiration as an elemental function is not to say that it must bear the same level of inspiration as Scripture itself. It could not do so, except to the degree that it replicates the Word and intention of Scripture. The Second Helvetic Confession famously says, "The preaching of the Word of God is the Word of God."[2] That might take things further than some would want to go, but it is certainly in the right direction. Safe to say that the preaching of God's Word grants the authority that the

2. Heinrich Bullinger, "The Second Helvetic Confession," Christian Classics Ethereal Library, accessed November 30, 2016, https://www.ccel.org/creeds/helvetic.htm.

Word has to offer to the degree that it is faithful in its presentation. It is well to say, further, that preaching that neglects the Word of God will fail to bear the breath of God. It cannot, then, be suitably inspiring.

Send the Listener Out on Mission

The focus of inspiration is *mission*. As we have seen, the means of engagement is story, the focus of instruction is theme, and the direction of conviction is gospel. The purpose of our inspiration is to set our people out on mission— the driving direction of the gospel in motion.

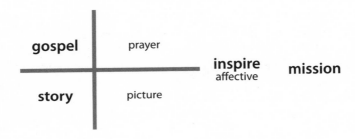

If preaching is filled with the breath of God, it cannot help but be on mission, because God himself is on mission. The whole purpose of the work of God in the world is to see the kingdom come on earth as it is in heaven. This, should you choose to accept it, is your mission. This is why we preach.

Every time we preach, we speak truth into being. We allow the voice of the Spirit to be heard more widely. We reinforce the way of the King, and we see the kingdom come. Speaking truth is a way of making it so. Of course, we have to follow with our hands and feet. The best preachers look for ways to encourage this practical response.

We want to see a world that is in keeping with the will of God. Such a world would see fewer women victimized by their husbands. It would see a more even distribution of wealth to those in need. A kingdom-like world would be less contemptuous. People would be true to their commitments. Enemies would know nothing but the love of their despised ones.

So how might we encourage such a world? How might we see this kingdom come? Some would say by political edict and social action. The answer, we are told, is to seek the influence and power that would allow for good people to initiate the needed change. This is not wrong. It is, however, incomplete.

In my early life I was enthralled with politics. I could imagine a political career for myself, and I think I might have been good at it. It would have been exciting to spend my life encouraging good and godly things from the seat of power. Over time I became more jaded. I have had many friends who have lived their life in politics. Each of them has done some good, though sometimes at an unacceptable expense. And some of those good things were quickly undone by those who followed them in power.

In time I sensed my calling was to preach. I have not regretted that decision. I have come to understand that the world will change as the kingdom comes. The kingdom comes as the number of faithful kingdom citizens increases. Kingdom citizens are birthed through preaching. Preaching the kingdom, then, requires that we call people to faith and faithfulness, and that we send them out on kingdom mission.

Prayers and Pictures

Mission is the means by which the preacher offers inspiration. This is preaching from an affective direction. It occupies the right half of the horizontal axis, representing the heart aspect of the temporal line. It can be expressed in terms of prayers (gospel) as it leans toward the objective, or it can be expressed in terms of pictures (story) as it bends in the direction of the subjective. The mission is the "prayer expressed in pictures" or the "picture of the prayer."

To say that mission is an affective element is to say that it is compelled by the heart. Mission is displayed by the hands and feet of an inspired disciple. Disciples take up crosses. Formed by the cross, they carry that cross to wherever they are called (Luke 14:27). They do it because they love Jesus and because they love the people Jesus loves. They do it because they want to see the kingdom come. They can see it in their mind's eye. They can taste it with their imagination. They can sense it in their gut.

Great preaching leads to affective response. We will know the joy of serving Jesus. We will feel the passion that is driven by the heart of God. Integrative preaching will not sit on a shelf. It will not be left on simmer. It will result in action—kingdom-driven, mission-focused action.

As inspiration leans in an objective direction, it expresses itself in the form of *prayer*. This describes how mission takes its shape as committed aspiration. Having met with God, we now make our expression back to God. Our prayer finds its form as an obedient service.

Our moment in the presence of God may have left us speechless. But prayer is more than just the spoken word. Whenever we respond to God with our words or with our actions, we are expressing ourselves relationally to him, which is the essence of prayer. Jesus spoke about how empty and vain the piling up of words can be. But when we are present to God and when we embody his presence with actions that display his love and character, we are prayerful.

To set ourselves on mission, then, is essentially to pray. When we embrace kingdom mission as a tangible and deliberate response to the grace we have received from God, our actions show themselves as prayer. In so doing, we will see the kingdom come in growing measure on earth as it is in heaven.

As inspiration moves toward the subject, it takes its form in *pictures*. This is about having a vision for the kingdom, where we can see the transformed future that the Word of God inspires. Here we speak the future into being by inspiring listeners to make real our vision for the mission God is calling us to.

It is common for leaders to formulate a vision statement for their church or ministry. Perhaps we need to offer vision statements for our sermons. What would it look like if the people were actually willing to respond to the message they are hearing? How would our world change? What might be different? Could we paint a picture of this missional transformation?

Inspiring people to mission is an essential, elemental function of preaching. Typically, preachers and homileticians talk about application, which is fine as far as it goes. But application is a far more limited term than what I have in mind for this.

Application suggests a simple two-stroke movement: teach the idea, then put it into practice. This is not improper, but it does raise again the problem of moralism. If preaching is merely about the presentation of principles that people must then apply, the whole thing risks becoming a mechanical transaction. Preaching can easily become a way of seeking compliance with a set of standards—a ticking of boxes that has very little to do with actually knowing and loving God. Pray more. Read the Bible more. Love your family more. Do more and be more in order to more fully comply with God's expectations. The whole thing can be very tiresome.

Integrative preaching is different. Having been renewed in the gospel, we then are led to respond in the same spirit—out of grace and not out of obligation. God's standards cannot be met by our obedience. They are satisfied only by his grace expressed in Christ. Our obedience is likewise built on grace. We will not be able to apply God's truth perfectly. Our obedience will be flawed—fatally so. But because of his grace, we will continue to respond to him. Despite the weakness of our response, we will still stand before him on the basis of his grace.

This is why integrative movement matters. God engages us by his grace. We learn of him through his Word. We are convicted by his truth and saved by his grace, which leads us then to serve his mission out of that same grace. Everything always is of grace.

We preach grace, and we do it by grace. Even our listeners' response is gracious. We will not be competent enough as preachers to demand their response. We will not be powerful enough through our own efforts to compel the response that the gospel requires. Yet our listeners will listen nonetheless. They will be gracious to us, and many of them will respond to the grace of which we speak. God will bless all this activity by his own grace, and the kingdom will come on earth as it is in heaven. This is the centripetal force of the cross-formed integrative model. Around and around we go, ever deeper into the center of the cross.

How We Send Our Listeners Out on Mission

Integrative preaching is missional preaching. Preaching is not about sustaining the institution of the church. Preaching, in the end, is not about us at all. Preaching is about sustaining and advancing the mission of the church. Preaching is out to empower the church to be the church—that is, to break out of its captivity to itself and to engage the culture with the Word.

The church exists as salt and light within a world that has lost its way (Matt. 5:13). The church is for the world, not for itself. Preaching, then, must mobilize the church to fulfill its mission.

You can tell when preaching has lost its way. You will recognize it when you hear sermons that call people to toe the line to a certain litmus test of expectations. When sermons are primarily interested in self-preservation, or when sermons seem to attack the world, preaching has lost its way. You can tell a failing form of preaching when you could not imagine hearing it anywhere except within the church's walls. There is a difference between loving the world and loving the people God created who exist in the world. When preaching builds a fortress against the world, it has lost its sense of mission.

Our preaching needs to call people to things, not out of rote obedience, but out of passion for the gospel and out of a heart for the mission. We will speak to people's affections, encouraging them to love things, to fear things (the right things), to find joy in things, and to offer blessing in things.[3] We need to call people to acts of social justice, not because we can fix the world, but because we are called to embody the character of God, which is to act justly and to love mercy and to walk humbly (Mic. 6:8). We need to call people to give faithfully of their time and talent and of their treasure. We need to call people to a set of kingdom values that arise from the heart first and then

3. Jonathan Edwards, "A Treatise concerning Religious Affections," in *The Works of Jonathan Edwards*, vol. 2, ed. Perry Miller (New Haven: Yale University Press, 1957), 24.

subsequently from the hands and feet. We need to set before our people a prayer and a picture of a world affected by the gospel and to call them to find their place within this transformed vision.

Great preaching inspires God's people to engage in the mission of the kingdom, sustaining the character of God as they engage the people of the world. Here is where the integrative model comes full circle. Mission moves around again to story as inspiration overlaps with engagement and heart integrates with human.

The mission of God is for the people of the world. The pictures we envision describe a world transformed by the in-breaking of the gospel. Preaching carries that gospel from heaven to human as people are transformed. It is exciting.

Preaching is supposed to be expectant. We do not preach in the vague hope that someday someone might be inspired enough by our comments to actually do something with their life. That is too much burden, too much discouragement, for any preacher to have to bear. We preach, rather, in the knowledge that God is already working to see his kingdom come. We preach into the flow of what God is already doing in his commitment to reconcile his world to himself.

We have read ahead to the last chapters of the book. We have seen a vision of the coming kingdom, the new Jerusalem descending from heaven, like a bride coming down toward her husband (Rev. 21:2). This outcome is unalterable. This is the trajectory that God has set in motion, and it cannot be dismayed. Preaching, then, is a most confident action because it is participating in this thing that God has already promised to do. Preaching that promises the kingdom cannot be disappointed.

On any given Sunday we might wonder about the response. Congregations can seem thick or disinterested at any given moment. But we are not dissuaded. The action of preaching is like the shifting of tectonic plates. Fundamental geological transformations are taking place, imperceptibly and below the surface. Every now and then we feel a tremor or see an opening in the landscape. Once in a while something dramatic will happen, and we will take encouragement from the evidence of God's activity. But even when we don't see visible response, we preach with confidence because we understand that we are serving the greater action of God across large expanses of time and space.

We are so small within the universe. What is humankind that God is mindful of us (Ps. 8:4)? It seems impossible that we would even be noticed by him, and yet God has privileged us to serve as stewards of his creation. Everything has been put before our feet (Ps. 8:6). We preach the mission of God for the creation of God in the confidence that this thing that God has set in motion will come to fruition in his time. We believe that our preaching is part of what God is using to do what he is doing.

Our piece of things seems so inconsequential. Yet like the proverbial butterfly whose flapping of its wings in California affects the patterns of the weather down in Chile, our preaching accumulates along with the preaching of all those who offer the Word in the power of God's grace to achieve the purposes that God has already promised to accomplish. This is no small thing. Never discount the effect of your preaching if you are faithful to the Word and if your sermons serve God's mission.

I have sometimes wondered whether preaching was God's best idea. Why would God trust his mission to people as weak and conflicted as you and I? How is it that the purposes of God could be put into the hands of those so frail as us? What if we are not so faithful? What if we are ineffective? Surely God could have come up with something better than this.

One of the perplexities of God's integrative purpose is that God has entrusted us, but not to the peril of his mission. The success of the kingdom will not make or break on the quality of our preaching. The purposes that he has set in motion are secured by his own divine authority. The kingdom will come, and that is not in question.

Still, God has privileged us to be part of the means by which he achieves these things. It is good for me to feel the weight of this. The kingdom is not dependent on the quality or consistency of my service. God's purposes will not be thwarted if I am unfaithful in my preaching. My unfaithfulness will, however, rob me of the passion and privilege of participation. There is no greater joy than to see God use me for his purposes in the life of someone else through the preaching that I offer. If I fail in my preaching, I still do not doubt God's capacity to achieve his purpose. The loss will be entirely mine.

How that works in any given human situation is harder to discern. How the Spirit works to ensure my faithfulness when a specific person's life is on the line is a mysterious matter. But in the sovereign stewardship of God, it all wonderfully comes together.

There will be times when God will lead someone to come to hear me preach. Led by the Spirit, I will faithfully act on my calling. I will preach the Word. The person God has led will respond to what he or she hears as having heard from God himself. The grace of God in Christ will redeem this person for eternity. I might not ever even hear of it. The person may not ever raise a hand or come to the front of the church for prayer. Yet God has worked, and all eternity is affected in result. The movement of the Spirit on my heart affected the heart of another of God's creatures. I cannot claim a victory because I have been so faithful. My faithfulness was prompted by God's grace. I cannot put a notch into my Bible because someone else believed. Their belief was entirely in response to grace applied to them. We are all just responding to the Spirit, and as we do, the kingdom comes. This is awesome!

Like many others, I have spent time pondering the face of Mona Lisa. It is her smile that is intriguing. It could go either way. It is an integrative thing. You can see in her a sense of chagrin, a knowing kind of smile that admits to disappointment. Or you can see in her a cheeky kind of pleasure, a confidence that falls short of outright joy but still presents as happiness. The truth is that how you or I see her smile probably depends on what is going on in our own hearts. The *Mona Lisa*, you see, is actually a mirror.

I reflected on that while standing at the Louvre during my most recent visit. There must have been 150 people jostling around the cordoned painting, and every person there held a cell phone camera above their head. Several were vainly trying to take selfies with the painting. On consideration, it was a little baffling. Why would you need a blurry photograph of a picture that you could download in high definition in a matter of seconds from any number of accessible websites?

I will admit that I took my own picture of the *Mona Lisa*. I suppose I wanted to affirm somehow that I was there for a moment in the presence of Leonardo's masterwork. We all want to attach ourselves somehow to mastery. In the presence of greatness, we want to know that we were there and that we have mattered if only for a moment.

The aspiration for inspiration lies deep inside each of us. We are all a little jealous of the Leonardos. We need not be. There is no greater masterwork than the creative work of God, this masterpiece that God is bringing to completion. We are the brushes in his hand, the palette full of colors that he uses in his work. Our words and our actions are useful for his mission as we inspire others with the gospel to fulfill his mission.

We will preach, and the kingdom will come, and all will stand and see in wonder.

PART 3

The Material Compounds of Integrative Preaching

Sermons, like anything else, are made of materials. Sometimes our building materials are well suited to the task, and sometimes they leave us wanting, but you can't build a sermon out of nothing.

There are a lot of things a preacher can use in a sermon, but in the end they all boil down to a handful of basic categories. A home builder will work with wood, concrete, metal, and glass. Sure, there are various kinds and qualities of wood and forms of metal. One might use steel or iron depending on the purpose, but once you know how to work with one, you are going to have a decent chance of success when you are working with the other.

Preachers have access to four basic building materials: problems, points, prayers, and pictures. Each of these materials might have within it specific functions. An illustration, for example, is a particular kind of picture. But essentially these four are the prime materials out of which the sermon will be assembled.

These four materials are compounds: each material results from two combined elements. Nature is filled with these sorts of chemical compounds, such as water, salt, and sugar, none of which are elements themselves, each one being formed when other elements are chemically united. Water, for example, is two parts hydrogen and one part oxygen (H_2O).

Homiletically speaking, problems are formed by combining engagement with instruction. These elements are "chemically bonded" in order to form this particular homiletic material. Stories and themes unite around a human sense of need. The problem becomes material for the preacher who wants to connect the listener to a biblical concept. The four homiletic compounds, then, are as follows:

Compound	Functions (or elements)
Problems	Engagement and instruction (E_2I)
Points	Instruction and conviction (I_2C)
Prayers	Conviction and inspiration (C_2I)
Pictures	Inspiration and engagement (I_2E)

In the next four chapters, we will work through these compounds with a view to the eventual assembly of two sermons, one from an Old Testament text and another from a New Testament text. The final sermons can be found in the appendix.

These compounds are a way of talking about integration. The four functions (engagement, instruction, conviction, inspiration) are not compromised when they are attached to (or combined with) another function. Our four compounds live in the gaps between the functions (or the elements). Each compounds brings together two elements without compromise. In so doing, they create a circle that is set in motion. As we move from one to the next, the motion becomes centripetal, such that the center is activated and enlarged.

9

Problems: The Preacher as a Pastor

A problem is a generative substance. Problems do not stop us. Problems incite us to more creative possibilities. No one motivated to a certain outcome sees a problem as a dead end. A problem exists so that it can be overcome, if we are sufficiently enthralled by the eventual outcome.

Up until the late nineteenth century, one such problem was the confounding limitation of physical darkness. Humans had more energy than could be expended just within the hours of daytime, particularly as they migrated farther north at certain times of the year. It seemed unproductive to limit one's collective capacities to what could be achieved only in the daylight. Fire was dangerous and required fuel, which was expensive. This was a problem in need of a solution.

Finding that solution took a long time, but eventually Thomas Alva Edison invented the lightbulb. This solution, which we now take for granted, was a monumental breakthrough in human ingenuity, leading to exponential outbursts of creativity.

Would we have unlocked the power of electricity if we had not been plagued by the frustrating problem of nocturnal darkness? Perhaps not. Problems cry for solutions. They are productive in that sense. Preachers need to harness this power of the problem as a prime material for their preaching.

Struggle with a Problem

The problem is a material compound of the integrative model. Like the uniting of hydrogen and oxygen produces water, a fusion of the elements of engagement and instruction produces the compound: the problem. This compound lies in the lower left quadrant of the integrative model, where the human moves toward the head. The subjective unites with the cognitive to create this material substance known as the problem.

Preachers do well to frame their sermons as problems to be solved because the generative power of the problem can be productive for the sermon. By engaging people through a confounding problem, preachers challenge listeners to move beyond their stasis toward a new and more redeeming future. The problem forces something in the listener. The problem creates a vacuum that must attract a solution. It cannot just sit idle. When a problem is on the table, we cannot help ourselves. We have to move toward an answer.

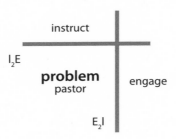

Just the motion of that movement is enough to spark the homiletic engine. We all know how hard it is to steer a stationary object. If we can get the listener moving, then God can direct us toward the purpose that he has for us. A relevant problem will demand that motion. It will not be denied.

Engagement and Instruction

Sometimes problems will lean in a subjective direction. The symbol for this could be E_2I—the problem as two parts engagement for every one part instruction. Here the problem will come in the form of a question. The issue will be more open ended. It will confound more than it satisfies, at least as the sermon opens.

This problem might offer a disturbing statistic or a difficult question. It needs to be something that digs at us or bothers us. We won't be able to sit easy with this until we have worked through it. We cannot be indifferent because the challenge is an affront to our settled state of being. In short, we are engaged, and we will not be all right until our intellect has been satisfied.

Why would a loving God allow innocent children to die in atrocities not of their own making without their ever having heard the name of Jesus? There's an engaging question for you. It's a classic—enough to make you want me to interrupt this book to try to find an answer. If it bothers you that I am not going to do that here, then I have succeeded in helping you understand the power of a problem. You were reading along quite contentedly until I threw that little bomb into your lap. Now you want me to deal with it!

Some other time, perhaps. For now I want to continue discussing the way that problems are engaging. Humans crave whole things. Brokenness offends us. Incompletion is frustrating to us. Preachers can use that to their advantage. By presenting something incomplete—something broken—we demand the listener's attention. It is hardwired in the nature of a human to not rest until a resolution is achieved.

Think of Beethoven's 5th. "Dunt, dunt, dunt, daaa." You've got to have the final "daaa." Try it if you don't believe me. "Dunt, dunt, dunt . . ." It's killing you, isn't it? "Shave and a haircut . . ." You can't help yourself. You have already completed it in your mind: "two bits." Now we all feel better.

Humans cannot abide dissonance. Nothing is more engaging than a problem in demand of a solution. So if we want to engage listeners and lead them in the direction of instruction, we will raise a problem. Ideally, we will tell them a story that leads toward a problem that is crying for completion.

Other times the problem will bend in the direction of instruction. Call this I_2E—the problem as two parts instruction plus one part engagement. In this scenario the preacher offers a *proposition* that is problematic. It is not so much a question as it is a settled statement, but that statement does not sit easily with the listener.

"God is sovereign over all he has created." That has been the big idea of many sermons, but it doesn't mean that it has sat well with congregations. This world is messed up. War, poverty, environmental disaster, moral promiscuity—do you really want to put the blame on God for this? If God is in control, a person might well wonder about the quality of his stewardship. We would rather blame people for all of this. Perhaps our environment would be in better shape if we weren't so addicted to our fossil fuels. The state of the family wouldn't be so challenged if men could learn to be faithful. Why would we blame God for all this? We are responsible beings in the world. Isn't that how God created us?

The preacher didn't raise this as a question. It was given as a statement, but it was deliberately provocative, and it was in the provocation that we found ourselves engaged. It is this compounding of engagement and instruction that the problem finds its power.

Preaching like a Pastor

Preaching through the offer of a problem is preaching in the mode of the *pastor*. There are many modes or ways of being that a preacher can adopt, and we will look at all of them. But in the work of problem solving, the preacher adopts the persona of the pastor—one who offers guidance and encouragement.

Pastors are shepherds. They work to help people past their difficulties in life. Pastors listen from alongside. They do not stand above the person they are trying to help—at least the good ones don't.

Historically, pulpits were ornately carved pieces of furniture that were elevated high above the heads of the congregation.[1] The layout of the sanctuary indicated the position of the preacher as one who was more advanced and more authoritative than those who gathered to listen. These days, we have come down some from our exalted perches. Many churches today don't even have a pulpit. Preachers dress down and use music stands. They do not want to communicate a sense of personal authority.

This is generally positive. We have noticed that the preacher is a listener too—just with the advantage of a head start and the responsibility of leadership. Coming down from the pulpit to occupy a physical position that suggests a more "parakletic" (alongside) way of being will be welcomed by the congregation and is more theologically appropriate. The way of the fellow sojourner is the track we want to follow as we occupy this mode.

Preaching as pastors means that we bear the burden of the audience. We hear their hurt and feel their pain. We understand the challenge, and we're going to help them through it because we need to get through it ourselves. Any problem they have is a problem we have. We might be a little more advanced in our understanding, but we crave the completion every bit as much as they do. We will walk together through this, and the people will love us for it.

I was recently at a memorial service where it was stated that our deceased friend had been "a better pastor than he was a preacher." I knew the truth of the statement, and I appreciated how it was valued by the people, but I could not help but think that I want a better statement at my funeral. In the spirit of integration, I want to excel at both of these skills. The truth is that great preaching is great pastoring. The two work best when integrated.

1. Kenton C. Anderson, "The Place of the Pulpit," *Preaching*, July/August 1999, 23–28.

How to Struggle with the Problem

We are going to have to take some time with this. I mean literal time—actual minutes in the sermon. I know we want to rush on to make our points. I know we feel the pressure to get on to the meat and potatoes, but we are not ready for these things until we have savored the problem. Whether presented as story, as statistic, or as a settled statement, the problem needs to sit there for a while. We have to carve out time and space to let it do its work.

Just sit there for a moment.

This is not wasted time. The more we sit on the problem, the more deeply we will value the eventual solution. A little pause. A little repetition. Perhaps restating in a different form. Just live there for a while. It will be okay. We'll get to where we are going. Have patience. We just have to let this thing marinate a little. The instructional parts will taste better if we do.

Several things will help us form the problem for our sermons. First of all, it will help if we know our listeners.

My day job at this point in my career is at a seminary, which means that I do a lot of guest preaching. People often think that this is some kind of an advantage because I get these great introductions. It is as if I have some kind of star power when I come in to preach. It's nice for my ego, but it doesn't really help my preaching. The truth is, I had more juice when I preached to the same crowd of people every week. The relational capital gained by living with the people week after week was worth more to my preaching by far than whatever cachet is offered by my current position and my PhD.

When I come into a congregation as a guest, I do not know these people. I don't know what is on their hearts, and they know that I don't know. I have to work with broad human generalizations, and while that is not out of place, it pales in comparison to being able to look a friend in the eye and speak the real stuff to them. You have to know your listeners.

Take your problem and try it on for size from the perspective of several of your listeners.[2] How would Emily feel about this as a single mother with her unruly kids? What will Kim think about this from her position in the corporate world? Chuck is unemployed. Natasha is on drugs. Samir seems to be holding on all right, but what if he had to contend with this? The better you know your listeners, the more sharply you can shape the problem for their engagement.

2. Don Sunukjian suggests the creation of a "life situation grid" that allows the preacher to consider the problem from a variety of perspectives. See, for example, Dennis M. Cahill, *The Shape of Preaching: Theory and Practice in Sermon Design* (Grand Rapids: Baker Books, 2007), 75.

Make sure it's real and not contrived. Listeners are savvy. They can sniff out your manufactured constructs. If you don't know where to find the problem for your people with your message, then maybe you need to dig a little deeper into the stuff of life. Perhaps you haven't adequately engaged this theme yourself.

You need to find the place where this message pinches. Where is the conflict for people here? What is it that I am struggling with myself? There has got to be something. This is the Bible. It always pinches. It always counters our natural inclination. We are always about ourselves. The Bible takes the opposite direction—every time. So what's the problem here? Where is the bind?

I recently heard a creative way of thinking deeper and getting to the root causes of our difficulties. It is called "The Five Whys."[3] It means asking "Why . . . ?" five times in response to a problem. For instance, identify something that annoys you. Then ask a series of why questions, one leading to the next: Why is it that you are annoyed? Because God is not answering my prayers. Why is God not answering your prayers? Because those prayers do not cohere with God's purpose for my life. Why are you praying for things that do not cohere with God's purpose for your life? Because I do not know God's purpose for my life. Why do you not know God's purpose for your life? Because I cannot hear God. Why can you not hear God? Because I am not listening. Keep pressing the whys. You might not need all five of them, but if you press yourself hard enough, you will get to what is really causing conflict.

When you bring that to your listeners, you will connect with them at the deepest level. I am not saying you take them through the five whys every week. That in itself would be annoying. I am saying that you bring them something that is deeply provocative. It might not even be something that they are aware of. Most of us have submerged our problems because we can't live effectively if they are always on the surface. We drive them deep so that we can cope.

But here in the sermon, we have been given permission for a few minutes to meddle. We have been given a temporary license to do surgery. So let's dig in and find out what's really going on with our text and with our message. If you handle this well, your listener will be compelled by things that she didn't even know she was struggling with. It might not be entirely pleasant, but it will be productive.

Preachers must see the problem from a number of perspectives, including that of those we disagree with. The easiest thing to do is to look at things from the most familiar place. But this is not the time to emphasize our safety. This is the time for courage.

---

3. "5 Whys: Getting to the Root of a Problem Quickly," Mind Tools, accessed February 15, 2017, https://www.mindtools.com/pages/article/newTMC_5W.htm.

So we will banish all straw men. We will accept the problem as if it were being described by our most fearsome opponent. We must state the problem so effectively that anyone who legitimately holds this opposing position would be honored by our statement of their concern. We will not win by framing problems in ways that we can easily knock down or easily defend against. We will need to make it hard on ourselves so that our preaching has legitimacy. That is the only way our preaching will have the ring of truth to those who want to hear and those who really haven't yet bought in.

Our listeners need us to have this kind of courage. It has to feel like something real is at stake. This is the only way our preaching will have currency in the culture. Jesus was described as speaking as one who had authority (Mark 1:22). That was because he didn't duck the issues. He went at them head-on. He loved to confound people. He didn't try to win their favor by speaking what their itching ears desired to hear (2 Tim. 4:3). They loved him for it. Yes, they killed him for it too, but in preaching with authority he saw eternity transformed. Whoever said that preaching was for cowards?

To preach like a pastor is to preach like a lover. We are not at war with our listeners.[4] We are not throwing problems like grenades. Our motivation is to love them toward truth. Speaking truth will make us vulnerable, as any lover knows. But the one who is loved will recognize the power of the truth and the spirit by which it is given.

The problem is a means of grace. The problem will demand that we move forward. It is a way of generating something better. God always has a better something for us.

---

4. "Faced with the prospect of rejection, many preachers have chosen to go to war with their listeners, forcing their ideas on people and lacing their messages with a strong dose of fear." Kenton C. Anderson, *Choosing to Preach: A Comprehensive Introduction to Sermon Options and Structures* (Grand Rapids: Zondervan, 2006), 25.

10

Points: The Preacher as a Theologian

The first and simplest element of visual design is the point. The point focuses attention on a specific spot in linear space. The next design element after the point is the line. With a line, one begins to express width and breadth. But without a point, nothing can begin or find a focus.

Points are especially productive things. A sharpened point allows for penetration. With a point at the end of a needle or an aircraft, one could sew a pair of pants or fly to Florida. You could even fly to the moon with a point at the end of your rocket. When John F. Kennedy fixed his intention on the moon, he made a point of it. "I believe that this nation should commit itself to achieving the goal, before this decade is out, of landing a man on the moon and returning him safely to earth."[1]

Kennedy knew that a mission like this would require the focus of the entire nation. His statement was deliberately framed as a commitment. There was a measured time frame (before the end of the decade) and an appropriate description of the limitations (landing a man and getting him home safely). By stating this objective succinctly and publicly, the president was now on record. He would be accountable for what he said. There could be no equivocating once the point had been made.

1. John F. Kennedy Presidential Library and Museum, "The Space Race," accessed November 30, 2016, http://www.jfklibrary.org/Exhibits/Permanent-Exhibits/The-Space-Race.aspx.

A point is a tremendously powerful construct. The point gathers the potential force of an object and concentrates it to a particular space or objective. The point draws the eye and focuses attention. Without a point, an objective will be softened and diffused. A blunt instrument can have a certain result— usually destructive. A hammer needs a nail if it is going to be productive, otherwise it is only good for breaking things up or tearing things down. But add the nail to a hammer, and something is going to get built.

Make a Point

The *point* is the second material compound of the integrative model. It involves the fusion of the elements of instruction and conviction. This compound is found in the upper left quadrant of the integrative model, where the head comes in contact with heaven, where the cognitive overlaps with the objective.

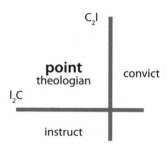

Points are essential to preaching. Until the sermon finds a focus, it will be ineffective. The preacher needs to know where the sermon is going and be able to articulate that in a cogent big idea. Without a point, the sermon will be, well, pointless.

As we have already seen, the biblical text may offer several points, but the preacher is going to find a way to focus the various points into one significant big idea. This we have called the "theme." But the preacher will want to make many other pointed statements. The more that these statements can be sharpened, the more effective they will be.

Sharpening a point is largely about wordsmithing. Unnecessary words will blunt the instrument. There is a humorous scene in the movie *Amadeus* where the king criticizes a Mozart composition for having "too many notes." The young composer is offended and has the courage to say to the king that there are only as many notes as is strictly necessary. The preacher needs that kind of confidence. Every word will pull in the same direction, and only those words that are productive will be included. Crafting a point statement, then, is about reducing the number of words to the minimum. Ask yourself for every word, does its inclusion change the meaning materially? If not, then let it go.

A point can also be sharpened by asking several questions. One question is whether the point should be stated in the positive or the negative. For example, we could say, "We should not be afraid of the love of God." That would be a negative statement in that it describes what we should not be doing. We could, rather, state it positively, "The love of God banishes fear," which makes a positive statement about God's love.

Another question is whether the point can be sharpened by a reversal of direction. In the previous example, the statement was also improved by reversing the direction of subject and object. In the stronger example, God's love became the subject, and our fear became the object. Opening the statement with love made a stronger statement about the objective.

Next, we will want to ask ourselves whether there are any redundancies. It is stronger to say "The love of God banishes fear" than it is to say "The love of God banishes fear and apprehension." *Apprehension* serves only to double what was already said by *fear*. We could ask whether *apprehension* is a better word than *fear*. We will want to choose the most effective word. The biblical text will give us clues. It is always helpful to lift our keywords from the text so that the congruence between our points and our passages is readily understood. Some words will be more vibrant than others, but they should be used only if they sharpen the meaning and don't point the meaning in another direction. The thesaurus is your friend.

At the end of the day, our points need to be sharply put and pointed in the right direction. When they are, they will penetrate and achieve the purpose for which they are intended.

Instruction and Conviction

Sometimes points will lean in a cognitive direction. The symbol for this could be I_2C—two parts instruction plus one part conviction. Here the point is designed to clarify and lead to understanding. The goal is to reduce fog and offer a more precise appreciation for the nature of the truth.

Often a truth will be self-evident if it is made plain. This is where logic comes in. Clarity of expression coupled with logical development of thought will result in a meaningful response. Unless the listener is deliberately obtuse or purposefully unwilling, a logical point, clearly expressed, cannot help but find its mark.

Logical development has two primary forms.[2] Deductive reasoning establishes a point by means of other points already established. This is a syllogistic form of reasoning. To use a classic example, if all humans are mortal, and if Socrates is human, then Socrates is mortal. The mortality of Socrates (the point) is established on the basis of the two previous points (the mortality of humans and the humanity of Socrates). Of course, some work may be required to establish the validity of the first two points. Logic builds. If one premise is deemed reasonable, then others that are added extend meaning. This assumes, of course, that every premise is warranted and that the flow of logic shuts down alternative possibilities. For example, if Socrates is a man, and if Socrates is mortal, it does not necessarily follow that all humans are mortal, at least not on the warrant of this one man Socrates. It is possible that someone might be a man who is not mortal. We know of one such example in the person of our Lord.

Inductive reasoning comes at things from the other side, beginning with observation of the world and then settling on a conclusion that seems sound based on observed phenomena. If experience shows that every human who has ever lived has eventually died, then it is fair to conclude that all humans are mortal. Of course, one never knows whether the pattern will hold for the next human, but the argument seems strong on the basis of the historical pattern. The argument develops from what has been observed and projects toward what can be expected from what we know so far.

For our points to be convincing, we must be as logical as possible, ensuring that the warrants for our arguments are fitting and that our conclusions are well founded. Showing these things to our listeners will help them. We cannot assume that everything we say is believable on its face. When we assume, we can misjudge, which means we might skip steps that are necessary for our listeners' understanding. Our points need to be clear and logical.

Other times our points will weigh more heavily in an objective direction. You could label this C_2I—two parts conviction plus one part instruction. In this case the compound leans in the direction of persuasion. The preacher is trying not solely to clarify understanding but to achieve commitment. This is preaching as proclamation—the presentation of a claim from a positive direction. We are on record here. We are not simply in support of the thing we are putting on the table. We are pro-claiming.

2. Alina Bradford, "Deductive Reasoning vs. Inductive Reasoning," *Live Science*, March 23, 2015, http://www.livescience.com/21569-deduction-vs-induction.html.

Proclamation is riskier than explanation. As we move toward conviction, we are personally invested in the outcome. We have chosen our side, and we will be accountable for the decision we have made. Our point carries our personal endorsement. We are taking these things personally, which means that we don't mind sharing from our own experience. We are not dispassionate about these things.

This is where preaching moves in the direction of encounter. This form of preaching is as much about introduction as it is about instruction—introduction in the sense that we are introducing not just concepts about God but the person of God himself. We are not just thinking about God; we are encountering God, and this exposure will mark us. We will not be the same.

Preaching like a Theologian

Pointed preaching is preaching in the mode of the theologian. Theology, when practiced well, is a dynamic exercise. It lives in the place where instruction overlaps with conviction. It is about the connection between faith and understanding.

It is important to remember that the Bible is not like any ordinary source of study. The Bible has an agenda. It intends to cultivate faith in those who read it. So while it is technically possible to read the Bible in a purely academic way, this is always in violation of the Bible's intention for itself. The Bible expects to change us. It is wired to get underneath our skin.

Great theologians understand this, but never at the expense of their scholarship. This is the beauty of the integrative concept. We are not asking theologians to compromise their intellectual integrity in order to embrace personal commitment. Both of these things can be true at one and the same time. These things can be integrated and must be.

Theologians love the truth. They love to dig deep and study faithfully. They are not intimidated by intellectual argument. They relish in it. They come with the conviction that the Bible can stand the scrutiny—that faith does not need to be supported by weak and inauthentic arguments. Faith and reason can coexist, and this is the work of theology.

Great preachers know how to work in the mode of theologian, moving listeners from instruction to conviction. We speak of God in the presence of God. We grow to understand him even as we encounter him. This is the point of our preaching.

How to Make the Point

The points we offer come from Scripture. The Bible is the foundational document out of which we understand the Word of God. We are not offering opinions. We do not guess at the work we have to do. Our challenge is to read the text and discern its meaning by careful exegesis.

To read the text is to take time with the Word, to let it sink into our consciousness and have its way with us. Certainly we will need to do the technical work of exegesis. We will need to define the terms, parse the verbs, and understand the syntax. Language works by a set of rules, and so its meaning can be unpacked if we play by those same rules. Exegesis is not satisfied with surface impressions, but drills deep in order to understand the textual significance in context.

What do the words mean? What do they mean in this particular setting? We will have to read more widely than just the immediate context to get this setting right. How does Paul use the word "grace" across the body of his writings? What does Moses mean by "covenant"? Having roamed more widely, we need to track back to this context. How would the Philippians understand the encouragement to rejoice?

And how are these words utilized in the construction of their contexts? Which words are primary, and which are secondary? Which clauses are subordinate to which other clauses? How do they depend on each other? What is the function of all the smaller words—the conjunctions, the pronouns, and the prepositions? "This, therefore this" means something different from "this and this." How do these linking words drive the meaning of the text?

What is the literary form of the text we are reading? How do we understand these different literary conventions? The parallelism of a poetic couplet offers different opportunities for meaning than do statements made as dialogue within a narrative. Some texts were meant to be read literally, and others expect a figurative reading.

Where does our text find itself in the flow of history? The Bible specifies dates and times and places that can be checked and ordered. The events of Scripture did unfold in real time. We must set the characters within their proper place in time while seeing all of it against the sweep of salvation history, which leads us back to see this work as theological.

We need to do the research. We will need help. Great preachers are not afraid to consult with others more expert than themselves. While commentaries might not be our first move, we would do well to read from trusted sources that can help ensure we stay on track. We need to invest our time in reading those others who have been here ahead of us. We will read from commentaries dedicated to our particular text. We will read from relevant theological writings that speak to the themes that we find in the text. We may even read from broader sources that speak to our issues from perspectives we don't share. The goal of all of it is to get the text right and to be able to communicate it well.

In the end we will find that we could say an array of things. These points will carry various levels of authority as they climb the ladder of abstraction.[3] Some of these points will be well and deeply established, with direct authority from what the text says to what we preach. To make the point is to describe the text.

Other points may move further up on the abstraction scale. Sometimes we preach with indirect authority: the theme we are communicating is biblically worthy, but it is not directly addressed in the particular text that we have chosen. It might be implied by our passage. It might be developed elsewhere in the Bible. When Paul encourages the Romans to hate what is evil, he doesn't get specific (Rom. 12:9). We could attempt to describe the particulars of evil as we see it, but we might not have full authority from this specific text. Some implications will be necessary, and some will be implied. Others might be a good idea depending on the circumstance.

The point is that a good biblical theologian will not overplay the hand that has been dealt. If the text gives it to you, then by all means preach it and do so confidently. But if the text is not so direct, then be honest with your people. It is okay. We don't have to stretch our texts to say what we wish they would say. That is where preachers get into trouble.

From a homiletical perspective, we must look for ways to take our sermons to another level. Noticing the theology in a text is a way to find another gear. I remember when my wife bought her Mini Cooper. She let me take it for a test drive, and I was surprised by its power. I was sailing along in fifth gear when suddenly I realized the car had more to offer. There was a sixth gear, which was an exciting discovery.

I love it when a point can offer unexpected findings. It does not take exceptional skill to exegete the Ten Commandments. "Thou shalt not steal" does not leave a lot of room for ambiguity. But we can introduce another level when we begin to wonder why respect for private property is such an important value in the economy of God. It is not entirely self-evident, given

3. Haddon Robinson speaks of the ladder of abstraction: "I have to be conscious how I cross this 'abstraction ladder.' I want to make sure the biblical situation and the current situation are analogous at the points I am making them connect. I must be sure the center of the analogy connects, not just the extremes." "The Heresy of Application," in *The Art and Craft of Biblical Preaching: A Comprehensive Resource for Today's Communicators*, ed. Haddon Robinson and Craig Brian Larson (Grand Rapids: Zondervan, 2005), 308.

that if we can successfully take something that was someone else's property, then we have enriched ourselves and have risen in the game whereby we measure worth by acquisition.

But what happens when we recognize that the prohibition against theft is in keeping with a fundamental aspect of the character of God? How much more deeply will our conviction grow when we are led to realize that to refuse to diminish others either in their physical wealth or in their spiritual being is in keeping with a respect for the image of God implanted in them? When we realize we are not measured by the accumulation of things, we can steal less and covet less and need less because we know we have been cared for in eternity by the God who controls the wealth of all creation. Theology helps us find that extra gear.

It is common for preachers to be criticized for a lack of depth. Whether or not they hear the critique, preachers often fear it. The most wounding criticism a preacher can be given is that the listener does not believe that they have been adequately fed. Of course, this might not be the most flattering metaphor for the listener. I imagine a crowd of overweight listeners lining up for a cruise-ship buffet. The preacher wants to provide a banquet. It is just that sometimes they lack the necessary stuff.

I have noticed on the occasions that my wife and I experience fine dining that the best restaurants do not serve the largest courses. If you want to eat a lot of food, there is no end of low-end dives where you can pile your plate beyond what is healthy. You roll out of those places fat and temporarily happy. The more valued restaurants do not mistake quantity for quality. The best places offer nutritional meals, expertly prepared and artfully presented. These are the meals that satisfy.

To return to the original metaphor, the sharper the point, the deeper the penetration. If you want to offer deep sermons, you don't need to overwhelm listeners with content as if to beat them repeatedly with a blunt object. A slender needle is sufficient to provide the healing medication. The sharper the point, the more deeply it will penetrate and the more power it will offer.

11

Prayers: The Preacher as a Worshiper

In 1901, Wilber and Orville Wright were disappointed in the performance of their glider at Kitty Hawk. Based on accepted aeronautical data, they had expected more lift than they were able to generate. This was a problem, and as we have already observed, problems are generative. Wilber and Orville were not going to be stopped by this, but they needed more information.[1]

I will admit that I had never thought much about the process that the brothers engaged on their journey toward flight. I have seen the grainy pictures of their original aircraft and have celebrated their accomplishment, but I had never considered what it took for them to get their aircraft airborne. Wilber and Orville went back to their research, checking their data and trying to sharpen their understanding of the challenge. They built a wind tunnel, shaped like a coffin, about ten feet long and sixteen inches square. It took them more than a month to get the air to flow in a uniform pattern so that they could discern a true result. Eventually they discovered an error in the commonly accepted lift-to-drag ratio that they were able to correct. This led them to understand that long, narrow wings produced greater overall lift than short, wide wings. In the end, the wings they constructed

---

1. Richard Stimson, "The Wright Brothers Get a Lift," *The Wright Stories*, accessed November 30, 2016, http://wrightstories.com/wright-brothers-get-a-lift.

were only marginally larger than their originals, but the new shape offered significantly greater lift. The result was that the Wright brothers taught us all how we could fly.

Problems generate. Points penetrate. Prayers elevate—they lift us heavenward.

Offer a Prayer

Prayer is the third material compound of the integrative model. Prayer integrates the elements of conviction and inspiration. This compound is found in the upper right quadrant of the integrative model. Here is where heaven reaches the heart and the objective is shaped affectively.

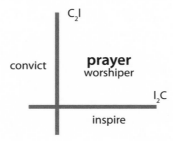

Prayer is a substantive homiletic material. It is not an addendum to the sermon—the thing the preacher tacks onto the conclusion of the sermon so that we know that he or she is finished. It is not simply an opportunity for the worship team to get up to the platform. It is more, even, than an empowering aspect of our preparation. Prayer is a fundamental substance of the preacher's work.

Preaching is a communicative act. It is God speaking to people and people speaking back to God. This is the very definition of prayer. Therefore, prayer is a way of being in the progress of the sermon. It is one of the modes or materials by which the preacher speaks, and it is particularly important at this stage of the centripetal movement of the sermon.

Prayer is the means by which the sermon gets its lift—the way the sermon elevates. We have noticed that the centripetal movement of the integrative model is coiling action such that the sermon rises as it comes around the circle. We are lifted from our humanness into the heavenly place. We have been brought into the presence of God, and we will hear from God. Conviction leads to inspiration and is given voice as prayer.

Conviction and Inspiration

Sometimes prayer will bend in an objective direction. We will call this C_2I—two parts conviction plus one part inspiration. Here prayer takes its familiar form as dialogue with God. Present to God, the listener offers the response that is appropriate given what it is that God has said. This is prayer in its relational sense.

This is an often misunderstood aspect of prayer. We typically understand prayer as a set piece, prepared in advance and presented to God as a kind of offering. It is as if we have been invited to give an address at a presidential inauguration or to present a proposal to the chief executive. We consult with ourselves and perhaps with a few trusted others. We marshal our thinking and shape our presentation. We then walk into the presence of the Almighty and make an offering of what we have prepared. We are not wrong in this, but we are somewhat misguided.

Prayer is supposed to be a responsive, relational exercise. You can't script your prayer any more than you can script a conversation. Of course, that doesn't stop us from trying. Whenever we anticipate a significant encounter, we try to work out the dialogue in advance, anticipating what someone will say so that we can form the perfect response. It never works the way we think it will because conversation is dynamic. No one is capable of predicting the exponential variations that a given conversation takes.

This is how prayer works. We come into the presence of God. He speaks. We are convicted. We respond. Repeat.

Prayer is a responsive form of dialogue. We never know how God will speak to us or what he might have for us. It always comes to us as wonder. We hear and our jaw drops. We contemplate what we might offer in response. We could not have predicted this. We can only respond to this in the holy moment that we have in his presence. So we apologize to him, we make requests of him, we worship him. We pray to him, and heaven comes to earth a little more than we had known before.

Prayer can also emphasize inspiration. We will label this I_2C—two parts inspiration and one part conviction. This is a more devotional form of prayer, the kind of prayer that touches the heart and reaches the will.

Whenever we connect with someone relationally, it has an affective impact on our will. It changes us. We might take a firm position on a particular issue, speaking strongly against another person's interest. But once we find ourselves present to that person, the dynamic is greatly altered. No longer is it possible to speak with the same vehemence. Our tone is softened, and our ear is opened. We may still choose to dig in and act confrontationally, but that will require the exercise of our will. We are going to have to want the confrontation. It will have to be the determined action of our will.

Presence changes people. It is true that technology has made personal connection possible from a distance. Direct messaging applications, video communication software such as Skype and FaceTime, and even relatively old technologies such as email have made it possible for people to collaborate and work without being in direct proximity to one another. Still, we have learned that there is no substitute for physical presence. Eye contact and human touch transmit nuances that just cannot be conveyed through a screen. Being present in the flesh offers something theological—an incarnational presence that affects the relationship in ways that are not replicable by any other means.

This is one of the advantages of preaching—physically standing in front of a crowd as a human being and openly sharing the Word. There is a vulnerability and a sense of human opportunity that cannot be managed through the publication of a sermon or even by the transmission of our preaching on a big screen across multiple venues. These approaches are not without value, of course, but they do diminish the impact of the physical presence of the preacher. We may choose to take such an approach for various reasons, but not without consideration of the cost. Moves like these require a decision of the will.

Connecting with God in relationship will similarly change a person, affecting one's deepest motivations. The element of conviction is about coming into the presence of God. Having been present to God, we will not be the same. Having been elevated in God's presence, we will act with confidence. We will be inspired to a greater place of faithfulness.

Preaching like a Worshiper

Prayer, as one of the material substances of the sermon, leads the preacher to act in the mode of the worshiper or worship leader. Worship is a responsive act. Great preachers will aspire to lead people to this same sense of responsiveness.

It is common for preachers to divide the interests of the Sunday-morning service into two distinct movements, one led by the preacher and the other led by the worship leader. The preacher, it is thought, gives attention to the cognitive intentions of the service, while the worship leader attends to the affective objectives. Preachers teach, and worship leaders sing. It is a neat and tidy distinction that many Christians have become comfortable with. However, as a preacher I am not content to cede worship entirely to the guitar players.

I am a guitar player and a drummer. I serve on the worship team at our church, and I am absolute in my love for this musical form of worship. But I am also convinced that the great divorce between preaching and worship commonly experienced in our churches has not been helpful to us. I believe that preachers are worship leaders too, just as worship leaders ought to preach. I do not mean that literally, though I do think we could allow our worship pastors the opportunity to preach on a regular basis. I mean that worship leadership, practiced well, ought to help us hear and respond to the Word of God, perhaps as much as preaching does.

Preachers are worship leaders. Worship is the intentional action of appropriately responding to the presence of God. As we have observed, having heard from God, we might find it necessary to repent before him, to be grateful to him, or just simply to praise him. These actions all describe what it means to worship. They all describe what it means to pray. In each case, meeting God leads to an altered way of being. This worship inspires a greater commitment of the will to the mission of God. Worship is not just an altered emotional state, although it can readily include heightened emotion. Worship is about the transformation of our being in God's presence—the very transformation that is intended by our proclamation.

Worship is a physical act. The word, in its ancient sense, literally means to physically prostrate oneself (Greek: *proskyneō*), to lie facedown before God out of deference to his glory and in humility before his transcendence. The psalms also call us to lift hands and clap and shout out loud. Humans are created as physical beings, and so worship needs to be a physical act—heaven touching human.

Sometimes a worship leader will call on the congregation to "forget about everything that is going on in life and just concentrate on Jesus and the presence of his Spirit." Whenever I am called to do this, I do not actually know how to respond. My Jesus is the incarnate Christ. I do not know Jesus apart from his presence in my world. To try to imagine a disincarnate Jesus is more gnostic than it is Christian. It is more about Plato than it is about the living Christ. We used to sing, "Turn your eyes upon Jesus, look full in his wonderful face, and the things of earth will grow strangely dim, in the light of his glory and grace."[2] I appreciate the intention of this chorus. We are calling ourselves to love Jesus and not the world. But Jesus came to save the world, and the purpose of his coming is to re-create the world according to God's original creative intent. He taught us to pray that the kingdom would come on earth as it is in heaven. The more clearly I see Jesus—the more clearly I look

2. "The Heavenly Vision," a hymn written by Helen Howarth Lemmel.

into his "wonderful face"—the more clearly and profoundly I see my world through his eyes. The better I know Jesus, the better I understand the world and God's intentions for it. Jesus does not lead me to escape the world. He leads me more deeply into his purposes for the world. My calling in worship is not to transcend the world. It is to see the world transformed.

We have been describing integrative preaching as a physical model for transformational proclamation, which is why the integration of worship into preaching matters so profoundly. Preaching, including its prayerful and worshipful aspects, must lead beyond its intellectual nature. Preaching is incomplete until it moves us physically toward the transformation of our will. This torsional movement from cognitive to objective to affective will change us, our listeners, and our world. This is what worshipful preaching does.

How to Offer the Prayer

Prayer requires that the preacher owns the impact of the message. Preachers ought not to pray only for the people as if this were some kind of benevolent action the preacher confers on others. Prayer is not a tool in that sense. It is not an external instrument that one can wield. Prayer requires personal investment. It involves us—it engulfs us. Even when we pray for others, that prayer becomes an innate part of our personal relationship with God. Prayer is not a button that we push or a lever that we pull. Prayer is actively engaged. We cannot pray and remain disengaged from the interests and consequences of what it is we pray for. Pray-ers are invested in the outcome. We own the impact of our prayers.

When Haddon Robinson defined preaching as a biblical concept that is applied first to the preacher and then through the preacher to the hearers, he was demanding this level of investment.[3] Preachers need to hear from God themselves. It is only what they have heard that they can share with others. You cannot keep your distance from these things. A preacher needs to wear the sermon.

This is why prayer is so important as a material aspect of our preaching, why it is more than just an appendage tacked on to the end of the sermon. The act of praying, according to its very nature, makes a preacher present. It moves the preacher from talking about God to talking to God. It takes the sermon from abstraction to action. Preaching that does not make this move is substandard. Preaching that prays enacts this active voice.

3. Haddon W. Robinson, *Biblical Preaching: The Development and Delivery of Expository Messages*, 3rd ed. (Grand Rapids: Baker Academic, 2014), 8–9.

Prayer in preaching is managed by an awareness of our voicing. We need to recognize the voice that we are adopting as we make our way through the sermon.

So often preachers adopt an authoritative voice. This is that preachy tone that people find so off-putting. That this speaking-down-upon is readily characterized by the term *preachy* is a revealing judgment as to how people in general assess preaching. We spoke earlier of how pulpits historically were physically elevated above the congregation in a not-so-subtle expression of the preacher's sense of privilege above the ordinary people down below. In those days, the position of preacher actually carried an exalted status in the world. Those days now are gone, and good riddance to them.

Preaching is a humble honor. It offers distinction only in that we are grateful to bear the Word to which we ourselves submit. The position or office of the preacher is probably more heavy than it is honorific, in that it carries the burden of a higher responsibility before God (James 3:1). It is not to be readily sought, because it is a weighty thing. To speak, then, with a voice laden with privilege is no more welcome than it is appropriate.

Preachers need to speak with the listener's voice, in keeping with their position as the first listener to the message. It should not be hard to find this kind of voice. To know what the listener might say if they were to voice a response is as simple as knowing what we might say, since, after all, we are listeners too. Preachers, we have said, are privileged only in that they have the advantage to hear first from God through the study of his Word in the presence of his Spirit. Having heard from God, they bear the burden to share what they have heard. This sharing, then, does not shift to the voice of privilege, like an emissary who takes too much delight in the authority invested in him by the king. Rather, the preacher speaks in the voice of the fellow traveler, though as one a little further on the journey. This is a preaching from alongside and not from above. It is a more welcome form of discourse, particularly in our current times.

Voicing prayer is a way of speaking with the listener's voice. Sometimes it is speaking back to God, a voice that questions, raising further questions or seeking further understanding. Sometimes it is speaking gratitude to God out of appreciation for the awesome things that we have heard. This voicing can emerge at any time within the sermon, when we pause to say a word of thanks or to express a word of wonder. It is a way of staying present to God across the sermon. This kind of voicing creates a more dialogical sense of preaching—that we are physically acting in the presence of God and that the relationship is real.

The Wright brothers were known as men of science and not as men of prayer. While they were the sons of a preacher, efforts to identify their dedication as deriving from their faith have not proven fruitful. It appears that the Wrights were occupied with the physical science involved in overcoming gravity. They were more focused on ingenuity than on inspiration. I understand this. It is this single-mindedness that often leads to extraordinary accomplishments. Yet I am grateful to these men because the fruit of their labor has been productive in the development of my own faith. To rise up in an airplane is to gain perspective on the world. Elevated above the petty interests of a deep investment in the momentary, we are allowed the opportunity to see the world as God does.

Humans are driven by the need to overcome the gravity that keeps us grounded. We long to know the glory that we were created for. Preaching is a way of getting airborne. In preaching, gravity reverses, if only for a moment, as we are brought into the presence of our God. The language of this preaching is the language of prayer. This prayer elevates us, and we are transformed.

12

Pictures: The Preacher as a Prophet

I enjoy photography and have occasionally captured beauty with my camera, often when visiting interesting places on vacation. My capacity to offer photographic beauty is limited by my geography. I can only capture what my eyes can see. Sadly, my eyes cannot see very far.

Perhaps the most beautiful photographs known to humanity are those taken by the Hubble Space Telescope. That these stunning pictures represent actual physical phenomena in the universe is hard to believe. The photos look like abstract art, as if they were rendered for little more than beauty. That the Butterfly Nebula or the Pillars of Creation are actual material substances seems beyond our comprehension.

The Hubble Space Telescope is one of the more significant ways by which we use technology to extend our physical capacity as humans. Our hands and feet are limited in power, and so we use machines such as forklifts and front-end loaders to multiply our ability to lift and load. Our mind can only think so fast, so we use computers to expand our ability to process information. The naked eye can only see so far, so we send telescopes into outer space to bring the distant to our presence. But even then we are confounded by our limitations.

The more we know, the more we know we will never know. For every question we answer, there are many more that we have never even thought of. Given God's eternality and creation's vastness, we are going to need some help in understanding.

Paint a Picture

Pictures are helpful in this regard. A picture presents beauty of which words can only hint at. A picture speaks of possibilities that lie beyond the surface. They say a picture is worth a thousand words. I think that might be selling it short.

Problems generate. Points penetrate. Prayers elevate. Pictures illustrate. An illustration is a visual depiction of a subject seen, remembered, or imagined. It is a graphic image of something tangible in life. Words bring precision in their reality, but pictures take things to a deeper, though less exacting, level.

Inspiration and Engagement

Picture is the fourth and final material compound of the integrative model. Picture integrates the elements of inspiration and engagement, bringing the model around to complete the circle. This compound is found in the lower right quadrant of the integrative model. Here is where heart overlaps with human and the affective is touched subjectively.

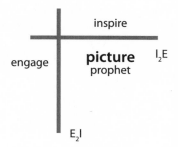

Several years ago, the Canadian government passed a law demanding that at least 75 percent of cigarette packages carry warnings describing the health risks of smoking cigarettes. These were polite little messages in stark block letters saying things such as "Your kids are sick of your smoking!" or, less subtly, "Smoking can kill you." The popularity of this campaign was so strong that the government decided it would double down, adding pictures to the words so as to deepen the impact of these messages. Now the packages have images of a diseased lung, a dying cancer patient, or a drooping cigarette. The addition of pictures greatly increased the effectiveness of the campaign. Of course, smoking has not been eradicated in Canada. Some people still smoke, but every time they do, they are forced to confront the truth about their choice. It is one thing to reject an abstract proposition. It is a much harder thing to deny the emotional impact of a pertinent image.

Words are exacting, images less so. But when word and image integrate, the power is undeniable. Words allow for a precision that pictures cannot account for. But those same words can seem abstract until they are pictured. When my grandson was born, my wife described him for me on the phone. But until I saw his picture and, better, saw him in the flesh, my knowledge of him was incomplete. Pictures are critical as a means of "real-izing" and actualizing truth.

Sometimes pictures will turn toward the affective. We will call this I_2E—two parts inspiration plus one part engagement. This is preaching by *design*, where pictures move with intention to achieve an aspiration. The preacher here is using the picture to create affective impact that leads the listener toward a specific outcome. The picture has a purpose.

Sometimes art is pure decoration. It doesn't have a purpose beyond the fact that it is blue or purple or whatever color goes well with the couch. I have spent many hours in hotel rooms but precious little time contemplating the art that decorates those hotel room walls. The purpose of those pieces is not to be contemplated. It is simply to create an ambiance or an affective mood. But that in itself is a worthy purpose, limited though it may be. The designer of the hotel room wanted me to feel at peace after a long day of business on the road. The art was chosen for this purpose—not to draw my attention but to create a mood of relaxation. If the designer has chosen well, I am more likely to want to spend my time there.

Art and design are integrated partners. Designers are artists, and artists are designers. Together they work to create a picture of an intended end. Preaching is also offered by design,[1] the design of the Creator offered through a purposed preacher.

Other times pictures will bend in the direction of the subjective. We will call this E_2I—two parts engagement plus one part inspiration. This is preaching by *determination*, wherein pictures allow listeners to see and shape some sense of defined and determined utility. The picture, as a material substance of the sermon, is used here to offer opportunity for the listener to conceive how the sermon will be useful in leading the listener to a desired transformation. The picture becomes personal.

---

1. "My subsequent efforts led me to the conviction that the answers lie neither in the traditional study of homiletical forms as forms, nor in a preoccupation with the vital content of preaching apart from the forms it takes, but in a sharper awareness that content and form are two inseparable elements of the same thing in the design of a good sermon." H. Grady Davis, *Design for Preaching* (Philadelphia: Fortress, 1958), v–vi.

Artists always have intention, but that intention is adaptable to the listener's response. Pictures are particularly good at not locking down the listener's opportunity but leaving room for the listener to understand its personal significance. It is important to appreciate the connection between meaning and significance.[2] We sometimes criticize people who come to the Bible looking for "what it means to me." The Bible means what it means. But until that meaning can be appropriated personally, it does not have significance. It is this opportunity for significance that an effective image offers.

I like to visit galleries, and often I find myself observing people as much as I observe the art. How people consume art can be as fascinating as the art itself. People at galleries are hungry for meaning. They browse the salons looking for a piece that speaks to them. When they find one, they stop and contemplate. They do not always perceive the art the way the artist intended. For some artists, that is actually the point. But when the design of the artist overlaps the significance for the viewer, something powerful has happened.

Preaching offers a particular form of artistry. The preacher is not content for the listener to invent an independent meaning. But the preacher is also not content for the listener to leave without achieving meaning. When the design of the text determines significance for the listener, preaching will achieve its intention.

Preaching like a Prophet

Picture is the last of the four material substances of the sermon. In this manner, the preacher adopts the mode of the prophet. Prophecy is a visionary way of being. The preacher as a prophet is speaking the future into being. It is about seeing the way of the kingdom as it comes into being on earth as it is in heaven.

Prophecy is often thought of as a predictive magic—Nostradamus on the pages of the *National Enquirer*. A prophet is thought to be a seer, one who can visualize what is to be, which would be useful in analyzing stocks or placing bets on the ball game. But there is nothing magical about prophecy, at least when biblically conceived.

The biblical prophet is one who speaks God's intention into being. Having heard from God, the prophet announces God's determination for the world so that the people are not without warning. Prophecy is a visionary activity,

---

2. "'Meaning' according to [E. D.] Hirsch . . . is unchanging once the Biblical writer commits himself to words, while 'significance,' of course, does and must change since interests, questions, and the times in which the interpreter lives also change." Walter C. Kaiser Jr., *Toward an Exegetical Theology: Biblical Exegesis for Preaching and Teaching* (Grand Rapids: Baker, 1981), 32.

but it is not a vision inspired by personal imagination. The prophet sees with the eyes of God.

The vision God has for his creation is a settled thing. It is not dependent on the prophet's effectiveness. Jonah was disappointed when God acted independent of the prophet's preference. The sulking prophet needed reprimand from the God whose purpose was not up for discussion. God's will is done. It is not a matter for debate. The prophet is his instrument, announcing what will be according to his purpose.

The power of the preaching of Martin Luther King Jr. was in his ability to see a vision of an altered future.[3] "Mine eyes have seen the glory of the coming of the Lord," he famously announced. King was a master picture painter. Consider the multiplicity of word pictures that he utilized: little black boys and little black girls holding hands with little white boys and little white girls, the governor whose lips were dripping with words of "interposition" and "nullification," all God's people gathering around the table of brotherhood, freedom reigning from the curvaceous slopes of Colorado. The people were able to visualize the future as King, the prophet, pictured it. "I have a dream," he said, and all the people dreamed with him.

Charles H. Spurgeon was a master of using affective, sensory language to achieve his purposes, often using words such as "See, Behold, Mark, Admire, Look, Observe, Turn your eyes, View, Hear, Listen, Hearken, Drink, Taste."[4] This is the way a prophet preaches.

The Old Testament prophets were famous for their use of visual imagery. Jeremiah buried a linen belt in the ground. After it had decayed and grown moldy, it was exhumed and held up before the people as a visual picture of their end. This is an example of how the prophet helped the people see what God was doing among them (Jer. 13). Ezekiel drew models of the city (Ezek. 4). Haggai built a house (Hag. 1). Hosea's own marriage served as a visual metaphor for the message of the prophet (Hos. 1). In every case, the people were led to perceive the Word through a sensory experience.

How to Paint the Picture

The preacher needs to be able to see the future, portraying its reality in concrete, tangible terms that listeners will recognize. So often sermons end with

3. Mervyn A. Warren, *King Came Preaching: The Pulpit Power of Dr. Martin Luther King Jr.* (Downers Grove, IL: InterVarsity, 2001), 129.
4. Jay E. Adams, *Sense Appeal in the Sermons of Charles Haddon Spurgeon* (Grand Rapids: Baker, 1975), 10.

a vague suggestion of some spiritual response, with listeners left uncertain as to how the event ought to have changed them. They may be favorably disposed to the message, but until the preacher leads them to a specific conception as to what must be done, they will find it easy to wiggle off the hook. Listeners are remarkably talented at escaping the implication of the sermon. It is much harder for them to do so when the preacher presses the point so that they can see what is expected of them.

What would it look like if we actually heard from God and were compelled to respond appropriately? How would we recognize such an outcome? Would we know it if we saw it?

The preacher needs to see it—and then show it to the listeners. What might be different about the way we gather together for worship? Who might be present who is not here today? How might our conversation change? What might we be doing differently because we actually heard from God through this sermon? Would our communities change? Would our business practices be altered? Would we have to change something or drop something? Would we need to adopt something we have been avoiding? How would our relational lives be altered? What about our families? This thing should change us. We have met with God. We have heard his Word. We cannot escape unscathed.

Perhaps that change could happen here and now. So much of preaching operates in the land of the hypothetical. We think of sermons as things that operate in the space of some other place and time—perhaps on Wednesday morning, when we find ourselves confronted by a situation that fits the scenario imagined by this sermon. Maybe then we could pull out our sermon notes, brush up, and thus know what we are to do.

That might be fine for that moment, but what about this moment—the moment of the sermon itself? What about an immediate response? Is there something we could do right now, before we leave the building, that would be a fitting response to the message we have heard? Do we need to stand up, take someone aside, and apologize to them? Perhaps we need to call or text someone. We all have cell phones. We could do that right now. Imagine a room full of listeners, calling someone to say thank you all together as part of the corporate act of worship.

Historically, we looked to the altar call as this kind of immediate response mechanism. This was good, when practiced sincerely, as a means of offering response to the particular call of the gospel for salvation. But there are a lot of things that we might call for in response to a rounded preaching of the Word. The idea of an immediate response is worthy. Perhaps instead of throwing out the concept, we could broaden it to include a greater number of potential responses to the message preached. Perhaps our applications could be more than hypothetical, about this moment and this time, instead of always some other place and some other time.

It might help to paint a picture of someone's struggle toward faithfulness as it touches on this theme. We could offer life examples of people who have made this message tangible. This is preaching like a prophet. Listeners will have little question about what faithfulness could look like since we have described it for them through real personal experience that they can replicate in their own experience.

Perhaps that example might come from our own life as a preacher. Reflecting on where and how these sermons touch our own lives is a powerful way of actualizing the sermon both for ourselves and for our listeners. We might have to go back a ways into our past to find a time when this issue lived on the front burner of our experience. Perhaps that recollection was more recent. Either way, by recollecting that experience and warming it on the fire of our homiletic stovetop, we can show our own humanness as preachers and offer ourselves as an example. Paul was willing to do that for his people (2 Tim. 3:10–11).

Focusing on human example will allow us to show how the theme takes place in life. This will be helpful for the people as we send them out on mission. The sermon theme intends to see actual change in the world. This is more than abstract hypothesis. This is about lived transformation on earth as it is in heaven. We need to see that with our mind's eye and project that to our people.

The truth is that people have difficulty seeing the world straight. In my case the problem is literal. I suffer from astigmatism, an optical defect causing blurred vision due to an inability of the two optical meridians to lock in as one. When the horizontal meridian is misaligned with the vertical meridian, as is the case for me, the vision is unfocused, and it is difficult to navigate with confidence.

We are back to the model of the cross again. The term *astigmatism* draws literal reference to a physical cross mark, as in Galatians 6:17, where Paul uses the Greek word *stigma*: "I bear on my body the marks of Jesus." The word *stigmata* has come to mean the physical nail marks on Jesus's body from his affixation to the cross. Astigmatics like me are people whose sight is crossed up, where the vertical and the horizontal are misaligned, just as we have been describing with respect to our integrative model. Good vision requires proper integration.

My situation is not dire, however, because I have corrective lenses that, when placed over my eyes, are able to dial my vision back to clarity. This has made it possible for me to engage my life mission with greater confidence. When a person sees straight, everything is possible.

The Hubble Space Telescope had a similar problem. The initial images brought back from Hubble were disappointingly blurry because of an incorrectly ground lens. Although the lens had been ground to an exacting standard, a miscalculation had been made so that Hubble's "eyes," like my eyes, were crossed up. The solution turned out to be straightforward, though technically challenging. A separate lens was ground and transported to the Hubble as part of regular maintenance. Like an eyeglass, the corrective lens was applied to the original lens and brought the images into focus, allowing for the clarity of vision that we enjoy today.[5] The result is that scientists are able to see much farther into the universe, in keeping with the original design.

This is the purpose of our preaching. Our sermons offer the gospel as a kind of corrective lens that fixes our vision such that we are able to picture the mission and engage it with confidence. This is the work of the prophet—the one who sees. Until we are all helped to see straight, we will not live in keeping with the purposes of God for his created universe.

5. Carolyn Collins Peterson and John C. Brandt, *Hubble Vision: Astronomy with the Hubble Space Telescope* (Cambridge: Cambridge University Press, 1995), 35.

PART 4

The Method of Integrative Preaching

Now we come to the actual preparation of the sermon. You have been very patient. Theory will not amount to anything unless it is applied. Our model functions somewhat like a map of the homiletical landscape. But models have to lead to method. Integrative preaching is as much a method as it is a model.

The scientific method begins with general observations about life, which are then formed as problems in want of resolution. Hypotheses are generated and are tested by the gathering of data, and these lead to theories that can be refined, expanded, or rejected. Theories that rise to the level of established wisdom then become convictions that will subsequently affect the values and visions that we pursue in life. You can see, then, how the scientific model traces out the path that we have chosen for our preaching: we start with engagement, which leads naturally to instruction, which grows into conviction, finally inspiring the desired transformation.

Each stage of the method pursues a particular product:

Discover—listen for the *message* to be proclaimed

Assemble—produce a *sermon* that can communicate the message

Master—make possible the *outcome* for which the sermon is assembled

Deliver—create the *event* through which the outcome is achieved

You will notice that each of these stages builds on the previous stage. The message is spoken through a sermon that achieves the outcome in a deliverable event. You can assemble a message or a sermon. You can master the outcome, the sermon, and the message. The end result will be delivery of an outcome, a sermon, and a message. Each stage depends on the one(s) that came before.

Over the next four chapters, we will seek to understand exactly how a sermon can be prepared. I will walk you through the development of the two sermons we began considering in the previous section. This is the application of our integrative theory. Real people are going to have to get in front of crowds of actual people with the goal of speaking transformation into being. Head and heart will have to combine such that heaven touches human. Prayers and points and problems and pictures will cohere, setting everything in motion so that the kingdom will come on earth as it is in heaven.

This will not happen easily. This will take time and lots of it, though a clear understanding of the model can offer some efficiencies. We will be vulnerable, and we will grow weary. But if we wait on the Lord, he will renew our strength, we will mount up on wings, and the Word will have its way.

13

Discover the Message

Scientific discovery happens in the most unexpected places, such as Archimedes's bathtub.[1] The English word *eureka* is transliterated from the ancient Greek *heurika*, meaning "I found it." This is what Archimedes is said to have exclaimed when he stepped into his bathtub and realized that the volume of water that was displaced was equal to the volume of his submerged leg. It seems a simple thing, but Archimedes immediately realized the value of his discovery for measuring and comparing the volume of irregular objects. This had been an intractable problem with respect to trade in the economy of the time. Archimedes is said to have been so enthusiastic about his discovery that he immediately leapt out of the tub and ran naked through the streets of Syracuse, looking for someone to share his newfound knowledge with.

I have never ran unclothed through the streets of my city, but I can affirm that there is a tremendous joy that is realized in discovery. Fred Craddock had a similar enthusiasm for his understanding of inductive preaching. "In most sermons," he said, "if there is any induction, it is in the minister's study, where he arrives at a conclusion, and that conclusion is the beginning point on Sunday morning." But why leave all the joy for the preacher? "Why not on Sunday morning retrace the inductive trip he took earlier and see if the hearers come to that same conclusion?"[2]

1. Mark Salata, "How Taking a Bath Led to Archimedes' Principle," TED-Ed, September 6, 2012, http://ed.ted.com/lessons/mark-salata-how-taking-a-bath-led-to-archimedes-principle.
2. Fred B. Craddock, *As One without Authority*, 4th ed. (St. Louis: Chalice, 2001), 48.

There is great joy in discovery, whether it is in the uncovering of a stimulating conceptual idea, a wonderful eatery, or a delightful conversation partner. These things might not even be new, so long as they are new to us. When we come across uncharted or untraveled territory, our senses come alive and our awareness is heightened as our consciousness works to embody a new set of realities. One can only imagine what it must have been like to be the first European to lay eyes on North America after many weeks at sea, or to be the first human to see planet Earth from orbit out in space.

To discover the gospel as an as-yet-unknown opportunity can be no less profound for the one who meets God and learns to understand his grace. The discovery of such truths is at the very heart of preaching.

Discover: The First Stage of the Integrative Method

The first stage in the process of preaching is *discovery*. We have now moved to a practical conversation about the actual practice of our preaching. The primary thing we are trying to do is to understand what God is saying and wants said through the preaching of his Word. But we must take a number of steps to get there.

In 1963 one of my former professors, Al Fasol, wrote a book titled *Steps to the Sermon*, in which he describes a straightforward process for the development of a preachable product.[3] He writes about things such as interpreting, organizing, maturing, formulating, and finishing. While the exact instructions are dated, I always found value in the idea that despite the worshipful, personal, and intangible nature of preaching, one can take a series of steps that normally lead to a sermon worth hearing. Preachers need this kind of practical direction, given the nature of preaching as a week-by-week discipline. Following, then, are my suggested steps to the sermon.

But let me say first that I know what you are going to do with this. If you are anything like me, you will appreciate the clarity of this instruction, and you may even try it exactly this way for a time or two. But you will quickly move on to appropriating these ideas in a manner that makes sense to you and works in the pattern of your life. That is as you should do. That is, in fact, what I do. While these steps describe my sense of best practice, I do not always practice them exactly as I have laid them out for you here. Rules like these beg to be broken, and I am the chief offender. I would only ask that before you get creative, you make sure you understand the intention for each

3. Al Fasol, *Steps to the Sermon* (Nashville: Broadman & Holman, 1963).

step so that if you wisely choose to adapt or abandon one or more of them, you understand what you are gaining and what you are losing. That way you can manage the outcome and still end up in a good place.

The Message: The Object of Discovery

The objective for discovery is the *message*. By having engaged this process of discovery, our intention is to emerge with a clear sense of the message, that thing that God wants heard among his people. Typically, preachers have used the words *message* and *sermon* interchangeably. I am going to argue that for our purposes it helps to distinguish the two. The message is the thing that God wants heard. The sermon is the means or instrument by which it will be heard. We can understand the message as the answer to the question, *what is God saying through this text to these people at this time?*

One implication of this question is that it is God who is saying the thing that will be heard. This goes back to our conviction that it is God who is the preacher. We are simply the facilitators for what it is that God wants heard. We are, more accurately, listeners—the first listeners—to the message. As we hear and are transformed by what God is saying, we have the privilege and responsibility to share that message with those others for whom the message is focused. We bear no particular sense of superiority. We speak before the people as one of the people, bearing the message that God is speaking. In that manner, the message can be heard as coming from God and not from any human mouthpiece.

The message God is speaking will be mediated through a text of Scripture because the Bible is the means by which God is making his Word known. Whenever we articulate Scripture, we can have confidence that we are speaking the Word of God for the purposes that God has in mind. As we listen to the Spirit, he leads us to a text—usually a particular text—through which God's voice is heard.

The specificity of the text will match the specificity of the audience. This is a message through this specific text to these specific people. We do not preach to *those* people. We preach to *these* people. The message does not target those other people—the rich people on the other side of town, the celebrities in Hollywood, the politicians in the capital. The message is given for the people gathered. If we have an opportunity to speak in the presence of those other people, we can offer them a message, but until they show up, we will speak to these people who have gathered with us so that they might hear from God.

The message is from this text, for these people, at this time. Preaching is stale dated, just like any living conversation. Preaching is a communicative act that happens in a particular moment in time. Time, like God, is in motion. We are pursuing something—the kingdom—that is emerging progressively over time as God perfects his revelation. Our preaching, then, speaks into some specific moment in salvation history, addressing the action and intent of God for that particular instance in space and time.

I remember the sermon I preached on September 16, 2001. I had completed my sermon research and basic planning by Monday of that week, but then Tuesday happened, and I knew that the sermon I had planned would not suffice in the aftermath of 9/11. Integrative preaching is not abstracted from the way that life unfolds. While this is an extreme example, this same sort of datedness occurs every time we preach, to some degree at least. This is part of what it means for heaven to engage the human in the context of our preaching.

The message integrates all these concerns—the biblical, the personal, and the temporal—in a specific expression of God's unique intention in that moment. We have otherwise described the statement of this message as the *theme* (see chap. 6). This theme will be distinguished from the sermon *topic*, the subject without its corresponding complement. The message or theme is the substance of the sermon expressed in a single sentence. We arrive at that summative expression by the following steps.

1. Identify the Textopic

The first step toward message discernment is identifying the biblical text and its corresponding topic. I have come to call this the "textopic" so as to put an accent on the necessary integration of the two.

We can work with any text as long as it comes from the Bible. The Bible is the source of our confidence. It is the one place through which God has promised to communicate his Word. To the degree that our message replicates the intention of Scripture, we can have confidence that we are speaking the very Word of God.

At times we will come to the message by means of a topic, and other times by the doorway of the text. It may be, for example, that we are invited to speak on a specific issue. We might identify a particular need that our preaching must address in the life of the congregation at this particular time. Or it may be that we come to a text through some systematic progress through a larger subsection of Scripture. Either approach is fine, so long as in the end we have a text for our topic and a topic for our text—a textopic. Ultimately, the topic will be expanded into an appropriate theme—the topic (or subject) plus its corresponding complement. The concern is that the text and topic are fully and appropriately integrated. The theme must express the text, and the text must give rise to the theme.

So, then, a church might ask us to offer a message on the subject of anxiety. That would be appropriate as a starting place. We will then go to the Bible to discern where in Scripture the topic of anxiety is addressed. Matthew 6 is one example. Our effort will be to discern a theme that expresses what the text (Matt. 6) has to say about the topic (anxiety) to these people at this time. Conversely, we could be working through a series on the book of Matthew. Once we come to chapter six and discover the topic of anxiety, we will need to develop a theme for the sermon that expresses just what the text is offering us. Either doorway is fine, so long as the result is integrated text and theme.

How we choose our textopic is a matter of discernment. Topics can be anything that seems relevant to the listeners and that can be discussed from Scripture. If we have a topic that cannot be addressed from the Bible, it may be that our topic is not worth the congregation's time. Or we may need to pitch the topic at a different angle.

For example, the congregation might be concerned about a specific item on the local political agenda. There may be no biblical text that speaks directly to the question of how a particular portion of the city is zoned for development. This does not mean the people cannot be helped as to this matter that is of legitimate interest to them. While there may be no text that speaks specifically to the zoning question, the Bible may speak to a deeper interest. Perhaps there is an underlying current of greed or indifference to the poor that is showing up in the debate about zoning. The Bible has a lot to say about those. The preacher could choose, then, to speak from Scripture about the more profound concern, while taking care not to overreach in application. The Bible is wonderfully principled, offering help on any substantive issue imaginable, so long as we are driving at the fundamental interests.

On the other hand, the preacher may be working sequentially through a book of the Bible. I highly recommend this practice. By this means, the preacher will simply adopt the next section as it comes up in natural sequence. The benefit of this approach is that the preacher is forced to address biblical interests as they come along and without prejudice. This can save the preacher some discomfort.

Early in my ministry I chose to preach through the Gospel of Mark. I was three months into my ministry in this particular church when I encountered the tenth chapter and its instruction on the topic of marriage and divorce. There was no way that I would have chosen to preach on such a subject at that stage in my ministry, except for the fact that it came up in Mark's sequence. I was able to preach the sermon, then, without signaling to the people that I had identified some special need for a sermon like this, because they knew it was simply the next text up. As it turned out, the sermon was widely appreciated by both married and divorced people in the church.

Preaching sequentially through Scripture is a great way to ensure that we are preaching "the whole counsel of God." It also allows for a deeper engagement with Scripture week by week. Every week builds on the previous, allowing a more substantive exegesis as the insights increase.

The tricky part here is to know how much text to take. My advice is to select a complete unit of thought, no matter how long or short. A complete unit of thought might be as little as a single sentence or as much as an entire book. Some narrative texts can be understood as a single flow of thought if observed at the highest level. Of course, there will be any number of sub-ideas or sub-subpropositions. Any concept legitimately derived can be chosen, as long as it offers enough material to preach on.

I say that we require a text at least as large as a complete sentence. We cannot preach an isolated word or phrase, even if it comes from the Bible, without importing substance from some other source. A complete unit of thought, minimally a sentence, ensures that we are discerning the topic and its complement. Of course, every sentence must be read in context. We must always work to understand how our ideas build from the flow of thought intended by the text.

Integrative preaching is expository in the sense that it exposes the person and intention of God through his Word. This is exposition with a lowercase *e* as opposed to various formal expectations we might describe as uppercase-*E* exposition, a kind of preaching more concerned about the form of the sermon than its intent to expose the listener to God.[4] Exposition in a literary sense is about deriving meaning from a deeply informed development of a text out of its human context. Exposition in a narrative setting, for example, offers the characters' backstories, the historical context for the scene, and the developmental aspects that have led the story to its place in time. Nonnarrative exposition is no different in that the conceptual material is derived from its technical context, including the human intentions for which it was originally offered. Expository preaching, then, is faithful preaching, deeply rooted in the bedrock of the text. It has not been lifted from its context but remains rooted so that the derived meaning never loses its original authority.

4. Kenton C. Anderson, *Choosing to Preach: A Comprehensive Introduction to Sermon Options and Structures* (Grand Rapids: Zondervan, 2006), 35.

This kind of preaching integrates text and topic. All truly biblical preaching is topical in the sense that it raises issues that matter to humanity. It is just as true to say that all biblical preaching is textual, as it exposes the truth of God's Word by means of the biblical presentation.

2. Read the Text and the People

The second step toward the message is to read—to read the text and to read the people. To read the text sounds obvious, so obvious that we might well overlook the opportunity. Before we go to commentaries and study guides, we must simply read the text—over and over until we hear it right. We will read it quickly, and we will read it slowly. We will read it silently, and we will read it out loud. We will read it in our contemporary language, and we will read it in its original language if we have the capacity. We read it with pen in hand, marking out its issues and its implications. We simply must give ourselves to read and not assume the text.

As we read the text, we also read the people. We must live among the people so that our reading of the text is reflected in our life together with them. We might consult directly with some individuals or with a gathered group, seeking the sense of the text from their perspectives even as we discern the places where they are roughened by what they hear. We might gather together a reading group, not only to help us hear the text, but to help us hear them—what is on their hearts and minds and how they see the world of heaven touching human. As our reading of the text converges with our reading of the people, we might hear from God within our moment.

3. Gather the Materials

The third step toward the message is to gather the relevant materials. Here we are talking about the material compounds of the integrative model: problems, points, prayers, and pictures. We can think of these as four bins that must be filled.

One of the biggest challenges in preaching is to move from message to sermon, or from hermeneutics to homiletics. This gap exists because preachers typically practice exegesis in a disembodied, disintegrated manner. If we think of our exegesis from the perspective of problem, point, prayer, and picture, the distance between message and sermon will be shortened considerably. It will be much easier to move from discovery to assembly as we fill our bins with materials already shaped as preaching fodder.

We readily understand exegesis, for example, as the search for points and propositions. It is just as legitimate, however, to think of it as the discovery of problems, prayers, and pictures. Doing so will automatically make our work with the text responsive both to heaven and to human, to head as well as heart. It will also make our study more compelling as we are presented with a more holistic form of thinking about the text that will engage us more fully as the first listeners to the text ourselves.

The goal, then, is to read the text with a view toward our textopic as we fill the bins with the materials that we discover. The resulting exegetical work will be distilled in material form as a problem to be resolved, a point to be proclaimed, a prayer to be professed, and a picture to be painted.

4. Conceive the Theme

The fourth step is to distill the message—in draft form perhaps, but in a concise and compelling expression that can be communicated well to others. The theme will be the unified expression of both text and topic. It will be a singular phrase, capable of expressing the substance of our preaching in a retentive and substantive way.

Such a theme ought to be as short as possible. Nine words might be too many. Two or three might be enough. Examine every word as to its essential utility. Is this word necessary? Is there an easier, a shorter, a less complex way of expressing this idea? How can we make it as pithy and as potent as it can be?

Brevity is one factor. Comprehension is another. Does the resulting statement say what it should? Has anything essential been lost in our efforts to shorten it? Has our attempt to be clever created a distortion in its meaning? Are there other words, better words, to say what is intended?

We must test the resulting statement, turning it over on our tongue and making sure that it says exactly what God wants heard. Of course, much more will be said in its presentation to the people. But if this were all that we had time to say, would the people understand the implication? Would they get the message? There will be further opportunity to work it for improvement. But to this point, can we say with confidence that this is the message that God wants spoken in this place and time?

Examples from Isaiah and Romans

It might be helpful to offer a couple of examples from sermons I have preached, one from the Old Testament and one from the New. These are sermons that I developed in the normal pattern of my ministry. I do not consider them to be pinnacle sermons—the ultimate example of greatness in integrative preaching. These are normal sermons, through which you might be able to get an idea of how this whole thing works.

One caution: this process can take hours and will result in a lot of material. Sometimes I work with a yellow legal pad, scribbling anything that seems of value. I can end up with pages of this stuff. Other times I will work electronically, recording and sorting everything I have in a note-taking application. What I am about to give you here are just the highlights. You can assume a lot of work went into getting to the place where I can share it so succinctly.

The first step, we said, is to identify the textopic. My Old Testament sermon is from Isaiah 60 with a focus on verse 22: "I am the LORD; in its time I will do this swiftly." The topic, it seems to me, is patience. I haven't yet said anything about patience. This is simply the topic that the second half of verse 22 is pointing at. My New Testament example is from Romans 10:15: "How beautiful are the feet of those who bring good news!" The topic here, as discerned from context, is preaching, or what makes for faithful preaching. Again, we have not yet proclaimed anything—just a simple statement of text and topic.

The second step requires that we read the text. I will leave you to do that on your own. I would just note that while both texts culminate in a single statement, you have to read more widely to truly understand. I would suggest reading Isaiah 59:20–61:4 and Romans 10:1–17.

The third step is about filling the bins: problem, point, prayer, and picture. This, as we said, is about using these materials as a way of managing your exegesis of your people and the Word.

As to the problem, Isaiah 60:22 raises the thorny question of how time works, particularly as we wait for the fulfillment of God's promise. The broader text describes a spectacular promise: "Arise, shine, for your light has come, and the glory of the LORD has risen upon you" (Isa. 60:1). This is proleptic language describing the future as if it has already happened. But it hasn't yet truly happened, at least not in the fullness we are looking for. It has been a long time—more than two thousand years. Are these texts just poetic nonsense, or can we believe that they are still coming true?

The problem with Romans 10 is that it describes an unexpected body part: "How beautiful are the feet of those who bring good news." This is not what we imagined, and it brings with it some troubling implications. Preaching with your feet suggests a level of physical investment that will be more demanding than what we might like.

As to points, Isaiah offers an oxymoron: "In its time I will do this swiftly." The point is that waiting on the Lord requires an expectant patience, a hopeful endurance. God will do these things when he is ready, and at that moment it will be like the work of an instant.

Paul's point to the Romans is that preaching is achieved with the feet as much as it is offered by the mouth. The gospel is a message, delivered by the feet. It cannot properly be offered at a distance. It requires an invested presence.

Now we come to prayer. We need to consider what we must say in response to these points as we engage the living presence of our God. From Isaiah, we might ask God to give us patience but that our patience would not erode into complacency. We could ask him to help us see the coming reality of his kingdom and how that ought to change us so that we are more proactive in the pursuit of these things. I sense this kind of prayer would be offered in a tone of humbled longing, seasoned with an expectant optimism.

From Romans, we could offer thanks to God for the incarnation of his Son, who used his feet to bring the gospel to us. If God had not been willing to enflesh himself with feet and hands and lips, we would find ourselves without the hope of the gospel. We might pray that our gratitude to God for his work would lead us to a more incarnational work of our own in making the message known.

Thinking in pictures, we try to anticipate what it might look like to embody these truths. From Isaiah 60, I can think of a specific example from the Academy Award–winning movie and book *12 Years a Slave*. I am thinking specifically of the portrayal of the slaves worshiping at the memorial of one of their fallen friends. Under the most abusive and painful circumstances, they sing of the rolling Jordan. They sing as if the promise of God is already made actual, which for their friend it is. Their worship embodies faith, which sees the future in terms of the present because of their confidence in the promises of God. This is a deeply resonant picture.

For Romans 10, I have a smaller picture taken directly from the text. I visualize the feet of Paul himself. I would have liked to have seen Paul's feet—sweaty and stinking, calloused and blistered, beautiful feet that took Paul wherever in the world there were people who needed to hear that if only they would believe, they would be saved.

The above material is gathered together and bundled into bins—problem, point, prayer, and picture. If one bin is a little emptier than others, it may be that we should dedicate more time there. This will be fodder for our sermon, compound materials that can be utilized in the assembly of a vehicle that will help people hear from God.

But we need to take a fourth step. We need to conceive the theme, or to formulate the message as a big idea. What does God want to say through this text at this time to these people? From Isaiah 60:22, we might say that God will fulfill his promise when his time is right. From Romans 10:15, we could offer that preaching becomes beautiful by use of the preacher's feet. Now those statements probably could use a little work. They don't yet roll delightfully off the tongue. But they will be good enough for now. We have a subject (patience, preaching), and now we have added complements. We have something we can shape into a sermon. We have something here we can proclaim.

You will notice already that preaching these texts is going to amount to more than just explaining the textual detail. We now are integrating the interests of head and heart, heaven and human, such that our preaching will not solely be about the cultivation of our thinking. We are thinking about things that engage, convict, and inspire, even as we think about how we will instruct. Our study has required a deep engagement, but it has been distilled into these single statements that we anticipate sharing with our people.

Archimedes was a practical mathematician. He studied ways to derive pi, invented the exponential system, and anticipated modern calculus. But his science was a means of practical discovery.

Archimedes was killed by a Roman soldier during the siege of Syracuse, his home city. It is said that he was murdered while working on a mathematical diagram because the soldier thought there might be value in his instruments. At his request, the tomb of Archimedes features a sphere and cylinder, emblematic of his greatest mathematical discovery that the volume and surface area of the sphere are two-thirds of that of the cylinder. This might not sound like much to you or me, but it led to a number of practical mechanical applications. Archimedes applied mathematical study to things such as screw pumps, hydraulic systems, pulleys and levers—the foundation pieces of modern engineering.

This is the kind of integration that marks the work of any great discoverer. We discover truth for the purpose of life. Our technical work results in practical application for the good of the kingdom and for the very purposes of God.

14

Assemble the Sermon

Complex technologies require sophisticated assembly systems. I remember reading a review of the then-new iPhone 5 in a technology journal. The reviewer described the phone as if it had dropped down from heaven in its current form. He noted how the phone appeared as if it were a single unmanufactured piece and not intentionally assembled from thousands of tiny independent components. This is the evidence of great design, that we might simply see a device for its intended purpose, unconscious of the manner of its development.

Good preaching is like that. If the preacher is doing well, the listener is not conscious of how the sermon came to be, what techniques the preacher used, and how the message works to shape the listener's consciousness. The listener does not need to know how, just that the how happens. The preacher, however, has to know the process.

Assemble: The Second Stage of the Integrative Method

Apple is famous for its super-tight supply-chain management system, which is generally believed to be the best in the world. At Apple, the right parts are delivered just in time so that products can be assembled as needed and on time. Contracts are developed with suppliers around the world who have dedicated themselves to providing the right part at the right moment. Contrary to appearances, Apple devices are the product of an intricately constructed network of relationships, agreements, and assembly and delivery systems, all designed to produce the expected user experience. We don't think about the headaches involved in assembly. We just enjoy the result.

All this is the legacy of Henry Ford. On October 7, 1913, the first Ford assembly line for the manufacture of motor vehicles was put into operation.[1] The assembly line may have been as revolutionary as the vehicles produced on it. Up until that time, it took twelve hours to assemble a single vehicle. Ford's assembly line cut that time to ninety minutes. Through careful planning, Ford's team was able to manage the task of assembling the automobile's three thousand parts in just eighty-four distinct steps along the line. The cost of a Model T dropped by more than half, to less than $300, making motorized transportation available to the masses. The world has never been the same.

It might come as a surprise to listeners that preaching has to be assembled, but preachers understand the need for a system of assembly that can produce a reliable product in a reasonable amount of time. Pastoral ministry requires a lot of energy from us. While we cannot shortchange the quality of our preaching, we must understand the means of production so that we can deliver quality every week on time.

The Sermon: The Product of Assembly

The second stage of preparation for preaching is *assembly*. The thing that we are constructing is the *sermon*. If the first stage was about discovering the message, this second stage is about building the means of presentation for the message. The message is whatever it is that God wants said through this text to these people at this time. The sermon is the vehicle through which this message is delivered.

It is this idea of the sermon as a vehicle that makes the Ford story analogous. We are building the means of conveyance—a vehicle that can move people from where they are to where God wants them to be. The development of this sermon happens as we assemble the various parts by means of a streamlined system. The better we understand the system of assembly, the more effective we can be in producing transformative integrative sermons.

This is not, however, a soul-sucking mass production. When Ford first started production of the Model T, there was only one color—black. There were no options, and there was no variability. The idea of customization came later, allowing for people to express their individuality through a

---

1. This Day in History, "Ford's Assembly Line Starts Rolling," History.com, accessed December 1, 2016, http://www.history.com/this-day-in-history/fords-assembly-line-starts-rolling.

number of choices. Now buying a Ford involves choosing everything from the seat-cover material to the fuel type to whether you want to be able to connect your iPhone. The product is variable, the means of production invariable.

The integrative preaching model offers this same kind of system. Sermon assembly follows a few intentional steps along the way. The result, however, will be unique, based on a variety of factors, most notably the text, the audience, and the particular moment in time into which the sermon is delivered. The system is repeatable and reliable. The result will be customized to the need of the moment.

Assembly depends on discovery. The sermon derives from the message. Having deeply understood the message, the preacher works to develop a vehicle that will drive that message home. The assembly process is about finding fit and finish. As to fit, we are concerned with the selection of the right materials, sufficient for the purpose of the message. As to finish, we are concerned to tune the sermon to its best possible effect. Fit is about discerning the best way to engage, instruct, convict, and inspire. Finish is about honing a sense of unity and flow.

The whole process must be immersed in prayer. This is fundamental to the assembly process. We have shown how preaching is a relational process, a dialogue with God himself. So it might be redundant to say that those who preach ought to be prayerful. Preaching is a way of praying. Yet often we forget the fundamental nature of our task. In every aspect of the process, we need to be talking to God, listening for his voice, understanding his purpose, and following his lead. This is all about communication—communication from God through us to his people. So we must pray, and we must pray intentionally. We operate with a general sense of God's presence, but here at this stage in the process, we will want to actually stop and be direct in our relationship with God. "Lord, what will you have me say, and how will you have me say it?" We have to abide in the Spirit if our sermon will apply itself to listeners.

The subject of our prayer will be the message. While this is what God is saying to his people, it is first what he is saying to the preacher. We need to hear this for ourselves before we hear it for others. So stop and pray. Praying through the substance of the message will help us to refine it. God might lead us in this moment to renovate what we have heard from him. It may be that we will find a clearer focus or more effective language for what God would have us say. It is good if this prayer leads to a more helpful statement. Having deepened ourselves in the theme of the sermon, we will be ready to assemble a sermon that has its intended impact.

Find the Fit

There are two moves in the process of sermon assembly. The first is to find the fit—specifically, to select the materials that will drive the sermon to its destination. As we have observed, integrative preaching features four elemental interests. We need to engage listeners through story. We need to instruct them by the sermon theme or message. We must lead them to conviction by the gospel. We must inspire them to the mission God has in mind for them. Engage, instruct, convict, inspire—these are the four things the sermon has to achieve. Story, theme, gospel, mission—these are the four means by which the elements will find their purpose. As we have seen, these four elements are managed by means of four material compounds that can be fitted into a sermon—problem, point, prayer, and picture. These are the materials by which the sermon happens.

So first the sermon needs to be engaging. The primary way a sermon will be compelling is for the preacher to tell a story that connects listeners on a human or subjective level. This story can lean in the direction of a problem in need of solution, or it can lean in the direction of a picture that compels further insight or investigation.

During the discovery stage, you will have filled your bins with various bits of material—specific problems and pictures that you will select from. The question now is, What would be most engaging for your listeners? What story do you want to tell? Is it a problem you want to introduce? A human example that will compel their interest? A vision that might attract their attention? Whatever you choose, it must fit the fuller framework that you are building into the sermon. It has to be something you can commit to. It has to be something that the listeners will be attracted to. It also has to be something that will lead naturally to consideration of the theme, which is the next move of the sermon.

You need to be careful here. It is okay to be picky. Try each piece on. Don't be afraid to set good things aside if they don't feel like they fit. You can always use a good story again some other time. It is usually best to stick with one such element, as stacking stories diminishes effectiveness. One of my mentors called this "skyscraper preaching," one story on top of another. The problem with this is that when you offer more than one, these stories start to cancel one another out in the listener's consciousness. It is often best to stick with a single story and to commit to see it work. The good news is that you are going to use only your best piece of material—a picture of a problem or some compelling story that will lock in listener engagement.

My sermon from Isaiah 60 began by offering a problem: my struggle to understand the nature of time. I preached the sermon the first Sunday after New Year's, when time was very much on our minds. Time seems to speed up as we age. Is that even possible? Prisoners speak of "doing time," which suggests that time is something that must be worked and worried. My sermon struggled with these themes that the listeners knew all too well. I used the picture from *12 Years a Slave*, which showed the people longing for the coming of God's kingdom, starved for his deliverance across the expanse of their lifetimes. God has made promises to his people, but he seems to be living by a different timeline. How long, O Lord, will we have need to wait?

The Romans 10 sermon leaned more in the direction of pictures. I described the hands of my two grandfathers, one of whom was a mechanic and the other a carpenter. You could tell a lot about these men by merely looking at their hands. My love for my long-passed grandfathers allowed me to take things to a deeply personal level that translates well to listeners. There was no particular problem for this picture, but the story set the listeners up for transition to the theme. I have small, uncalloused preacher hands. It is a good thing that preachers are not judged by their hands. Preachers are judged by their feet.

Having engaged the listener, the second move of the sermon is to instruct. Instruction happens as we work with points and problems. This is where we establish the sermon theme, the point that speaks to the problem. This is where the listener hears the message—that thing that God wants heard through this text to these people at this time.

You have choices here. You can act more pastorally, helping the listeners appreciate a biblical approach to a personal or human challenge. Or you can take the role of the theologian, encouraging them to a deepened appreciation of the will and way of God. The question is, Which will be the most instructive for your listeners? Which approach will take them further and help them most in this specific instance?

My Romans 10 sermon leaned toward the latter approach. During the discovery stage, I had stated the theme of the sermon as follows: "Preaching becomes beautiful by use of the preacher's feet." Having given this a little thought, I knew I could improve it. I tried on a few possibilities. "Beautiful preachers use their feet." "Beautiful feet make for beautiful preaching." The challenge here is to make a theological statement that will ring in the ears and make the point unforgettable. I made heavy use of my online thesaurus. Redundant words or words that might misdirect had to be eliminated, sometimes reluctantly. I needed fewer words, but enough words. I needed words that would sing, words that would shine. It is a lot to ask. But the better the theme, the more effective the sermon. I settled on "Preaching is feet first."

I stewed over whether to use the word *beautiful*, but in the end I determined that the objective of the text was not to offer something beautiful. The goal of the text was to encourage an effective preaching of the gospel. We could call the result of this preaching beautiful, but the production of beauty is secondary. One could argue that the feet aspect of the text was also not primary, but I would disagree. Not only do feet offer great imagery for the sermon, but the image drives the theological angle, that preaching is an intentional and incarnational action. Good theology always makes a sermon stronger.

This theme, then, offers the substance of the sermon's instruction. We will have to show that preaching with the feet means that our preaching will be (a) intentional (we never use our feet by accident) and (b) incarnational (feet always move us physically). In the alliterative spirit, we could add that this preaching will be (c) impressionable, in that feet always leave a footprint, but perhaps this one is a more tenuous implication of the text. We are not simply considering the natural result of using feet. The intentional and incarnational aspects are driven by the contextual call, "How can they hear without a preacher?" The sermon now will need to show this to the listeners so that they are convinced of the fact that the most effective, most beautiful preaching will first require that preachers use their feet.

The Isaiah 60 sermon, conversely, leans a little closer to the pastoral, though not without attention to theology. We have seen that the message or theme of the sermon was "God will fulfill his promise when the time is right." I pressed that further, settling on "God is urgent for his promise within the timing of his purpose." I liked the way this statement expressed the patient expectation required by the text. I also liked the way it rolled off the tongue. I could imagine almost singing this statement in the context of the sermon.

This is certainly a theological point, connecting God's promise with his purpose. But it is oriented as a response to the listeners' natural impatience. It is hard to wait when God seems so inactive. But this theme suggests that God brings urgency to everything he does, but always within the timing of his greater purpose. This will require some instruction in how the Bible speaks of time—*kairos* time, which appreciates the rightness of a moment.

In both of these sermons, the challenge is to lead listeners to a different cognitive place. We want to deepen their understanding of biblical truth, in the former case with respect to incarnation and in the latter case with respect to an urgent patience. These truths will not be easily appropriated, and we will not be able to get there without establishing theological understanding.

The third movement of the sermon is to bring the listeners to a place of conviction. It is not enough simply that they understand. They now have to be led to commitment in the presence of God. We have comprehended truth. Now it is time to see whether we can embody and obey it. This is where theology turns to worship—where the point produces prayer. This is going to require a hearing of the gospel.

I am amazed how often preachers believe that they have done their job when they have achieved mere understanding. Anybody can understand biblical truth. Even the demons believe this stuff (James 2:19). Preachers teach truth and then stop, believing they have made their point. They may have clarified the truth, but that does not mean that anyone is yet ready to give their life for it, to sell everything they have and give it to the poor, to change the fundamental coding of their base being. This is about moving from instruction to conviction, and that will only happen as the listeners are led to meet with God. It is the encounter with the living God that will transform them. It is seeing how the gospel elevates the sermon.

The text for my Isaiah sermon offered a convenient way of getting there. Sometimes we need to keep reading the context of the text. In this case, chapter 61 opens with familiar words: "The Spirit of the Sovereign LORD is on me, because the LORD has anointed me to proclaim good news to the poor." If these words sound familiar, it is because we have heard them before. These are the words that Jesus read in the temple (Luke 4:18). It was by these words that Jesus presented himself as the fulfillment of God's Isaiah 60 promise. Jesus came in the fullness of time (Gal. 4:4). This was that time—God's time, *kairos* time, gospel time! In the fullness of time, when Jesus came, it was like the work of a moment.

And now we await another time, but we do so with the advantage of knowing that God has already shown himself faithful to his promise within the timing of his purpose. It allows for us to be patient in our expectation of our Lord's second coming. Isaiah 61 allows listeners to move from instruction to conviction. Because we have seen Jesus and have received his grace, we know that we will see him once again. In his time he will do this quickly, just like he did the first time. The prayer the preacher offers will be obvious at this point: even so, Lord Jesus, come quickly.

That preaching is feet first also requires a movement to conviction. I can accept this intellectually, but that doesn't mean that I like it. I would have preferred it if the text said "mouth." How beautiful are the lips, the teeth, the throat of the one who brings good news. I am pretty good with my mouth. I can talk. I know how to speak the gospel, and I can do it from a distance. I can broadcast the gospel, blog the gospel, tweet the gospel, not that there is anything wrong with that. But as long as I use my mouth, I can keep my distance. Until I preach with my feet, I have not met the listener. I have not yet been incarnational. I have not yet been like Jesus.

I will need to lead the listeners to appreciate the way that Jesus used his feet—the fact that Jesus had feet, actually, and that he was and is more than just some impersonal force or inclination. Jesus met us in the flesh. He brought truth to us, and he did it with his feet. Using our feet makes us vulnerable. In Jesus's case, it cost him his very life. They put nails through his beautiful feet, and in result we have everlasting hope. This is where the sermon offers gospel. This is where the sermon shapes conviction.

This is a big moment in the movement of the sermon. The listeners have a lot to say to God at a point like this, and it is the preacher's job to lead them in this moment of confession. We are vulnerable here, and we need to own this so that the conviction deepens. "Lord, we are sorry for the fear that has kept us from using our feet. We are worried that our desire to keep our distance has meant that others have not had the opportunity to hear. Forgive us for our apathy and lethargy and for all those things that have kept our preaching feetless. Forgive us for the arrogance that has led us to believe that our mouths are adequate. Give us the courage to use our feet. And thank you, Lord, for using yours."

Our final move offers inspiration. Having been engaged, we were open to instruction. Having been instructed, we were moved toward conviction. Having come to conviction, we are ready to be inspired to mission.

David Buttrick speaks of how sermons need to form in consciousness—how the structure of the sermon needs to move.[2] The integrative preaching model has embraced this sense of movement. The sermon now has come full circle. It is coiling toward the trajectory of the gospel. We are transformed by this gospel, and the world itself will be transformed. The sermon has not kept us static. We have come to a new and different place because of our engagement with the world.

This is what makes preaching missional—the sense that preaching has a purpose to fulfill. This final challenge for the preacher is to understand how conviction will inspire a God-directed change. What would this change look like? How might we recognize the difference that this theme was constructed to achieve? What could we do with this sermon to actualize this sense of mission? This will be more than what the preacher says. It will be about what we do together and how we can imagine the necessary change. Integrative preaching is a physical model of transformational proclamation. This thing has to actually move us somewhere.

Our feet sermon is a natural in this regard. We have the example of Paul's stinking, sweaty, swelling feet, made beautiful by his willingness to make

2. David Buttrick, "Developing Moves," in *Homiletic: Moves and Structures* (Philadelphia: Fortress, 1987), 37–53.

himself present to the people who needed to hear his message of salvation. When was the last time we really used our feet? When and how have we made ourselves present? What would it look like if you and I used our feet? How might that be beautiful?

Usually when a sermon is over, people will stand up on their feet and put one of those feet in front of the other, propelling themselves to some other place, often home or to a restaurant. The problem here is that once the listeners use their feet, the preacher loses control of the situation. We cannot follow every listener to see where they go.

In the end, the preacher always has to trust listeners to make their own response before their Lord. The truth is, they might choose not to. The hard fact is that sometimes listeners say no. Sometimes they fail to act on the Word. This is disappointing when it happens, but as preachers we know we are in good company. People said no to Jesus. They were willing to walk away from the Word. But this will not stop us from trying to be inspiring. We will not let our listeners wiggle out too easily. We will be as clear and as practical as we can in painting the picture of what this thing will look like.

From Isaiah 60 we need to learn how to be patient without losing our sense of expectation. To help listeners appreciate this, I told them a personal story about a time before my wife and I were married. She had decided to spend a month in England with her friend. I have seldom known such loneliness. If there were ever a question whether she was the woman I would marry, it was settled by this time of separation. I bought a calendar and put it on the wall, crossing off every day as it passed. The passage of time had never seemed so slow. I had to work at being patient, because my expectation was so overwhelming. I lived for the expectation to the point that it would have damaged me if I was not able to find the patience that the waiting required. When Karen returned, my life and world were restored. It was like the work of an instant. As soon as she was back, it was like the time had never happened, except for the fact that it had happened and that I had been changed by it—I had been deepened by it.

For now we suffer in the world, and it is not easy for those called to a higher kingdom. The world doesn't get us. It seems we are misfits, having been fitted for a better, more eternal world. We wait for heaven, and it feels like it may never come. Every aspect of our being longs for, cries for the coming of Christ's kingdom. It is not here yet, and so we wait with patient expectation, knowing that when it does come, it will be like the work of an instant. We will be changed, and we will be all that God has prepared for us to be.

So the challenge now is that we wait. This is not the most inspiring challenge. We wait patiently for now, but with a sense of expectation. We continue to seek the kingdom here on earth as it is in heaven, until the day he comes again. It is sometimes an uncomfortable fit. We get hit on one side of the face, and we make available the other. Patience does not mean we won't get hurt. But our conviction is that the King is coming, and that conviction inspires us to a patient expectation.

Apply the Finish

So far we have built a structure for our sermon—four moves that engage a theme such that conviction inspires transformation. The materials have been assembled such that the elements all find their place in the resulting sermon. Everything fits. Now it's time to apply the finish.

Sermon finishing is about considering unity and flow. Unity is about making sure the imagery and language are consistent throughout. Flow is about making sure there is no unnecessary material, while ensuring there is enough, so that the sermon is well paced, allowing the listener time to experience the transformational process.

A sermon that has unity is a sermon in which everything is moving in the same direction. This does not necessarily mean that everything is linear. There may be compelling reasons to mess around with order, so long as all the elements are present.[3] But everything that is going on in the sermon, particularly its language and its imagery, ought to be locked into a unified purpose. You do not want to be chasing rabbits or following digressions, because these things will fracture consciousness and threaten the listener's engagement with your message.

Locking in the language will help to ensure that the ideas of the sermon retain a sense of unity. The best way to do this is to commit to the language offered by the sermon theme. The theme of my Romans sermon is that preaching is feet first. So throughout the sermon I will use the language that this theme offers. I will speak about preaching with the feet—how preaching can't be offered with the mouth until it is propelled by the feet. I will talk about lazy feet and blistered feet and beautiful feet—how feet make preaching incarnational and intentional. I will keep driving this language till I am certain that my listeners will be dreaming about feet when they place their head on the pillow and will be singing about feet when they take their morning shower.

Repetition is the listener's friend. If you don't believe that, listen to pop music and recognize how catchy the linguistic hook is. Or consider more highbrow forms of music. Both classical and jazz music allow a song to wander

3. Kenton C. Anderson, *Choosing to Preach: A Comprehensive Introduction to Sermon Options and Structures* (Grand Rapids: Zondervan, 2006), 254.

widely so long as it always returns to the musical theme. It is the theme that gives the piece its unity.

The Isaiah 60 theme was that God is urgent for his promise within the timing of his purpose. This sermon will be thick with language about promises and purposes. I will talk incessantly of time. God will take his time, but when it's time, we will know his purpose. His promise will come in time—his time—when the time is perfect for his purpose. It's time we were patient. Expect his promise in his time. As long as we are in time, there is still time for his purpose to be fulfilled. He has promised us his time and promised that there will be enough time for us to see his purpose in his time. The sermon will have unity because the language is all of a piece. My repetition of this language will ensure that listeners will not be able to forget the theme the sermon offers.

The other way to ensure unity is to use consistent imagery. So many sermons offer an array of images. There might be a story about football followed by a metaphor from politics. This is followed by a quotation from church history. That could work if all the images had a common character, but most often they do not. Great sermons will work to ensure that there is a common hue or consistent palette to all the imagery that the sermon offers.

Every image, metaphor, and visionary aspect of my Isaiah 60 sermon will have some way of picturing time. I will talk about the elasticity of time. I will speak of prisoners and slaves "doing time." I will picture Jesus sitting down after reading from the scroll, waiting till the people recognized that the time of the Scripture's promise was now. I will describe myself marking squares on the calendar. If I can't show a relationship to time, I will not use the image because it will only get in the way. This family of images will give the sermon unity and make it memorable.

From Romans 10, I will make constant and consistent use of feet. I will contrast feet with my grandfathers' hands. I will talk about getting up in the morning and standing to my feet, putting one foot in front of the other in an intentional act. I will talk about how feet leave footprints and how they always make a person present. I will talk about how it is easier to use the tongue than the feet, and I will imagine Paul's and Jesus's feet. I might even take my shoes and socks off so as to examine my own feet (probably not). That would be sure to make the sermon stick. There will not be a visual aspect of the sermon that cannot be connected to the feet, because that is what the biblical text gave me, and that is what will help to unite the sermon as a single and powerful expression. If it doesn't fit, it will not finish.

Sermon flow, or pacing, is the second aspect of putting finish to the sermon. Every sermon exists across a space of time. How much time is irrelevant. I know that some people believe you cannot preach a great sermon in less than forty-five minutes. They are wrong. I have heard sermons that changed my life that were not more than eight or nine minutes. I have sat spellbound listening to sermons that lasted at least an hour. The amount of time is not material. Of course, you can say more over longer periods of time, but saying more does not necessarily make for better preaching. Sometimes preachers will have a greater impact if they say less—a lot less.

Time matters in preaching, but not in the way we think. It is not the amount of time but how the time is spent. Eugene Lowry wrote an excellent book on the subject, so helpful that you only need to read the title to get the point: *Doing Time in the Pulpit*.[4] The point is that time is something that needs to be worked. However much time you have, you must allocate your use of that time for the purposes that you intend.

The preacher who runs out of time, cramming the final point into the final moments, is lazy. This preacher has not given consideration to the way time works. Again, it is not our goal to fill the time with as much content as possible. If so, great preachers would speak like auctioneers or high school debaters, accelerating their speech to increase the word count. Less is more—always so. Great design in preaching will feature plenty of white space because our words have to breathe if they will have impact. Listeners need time to hear what we have to say so that they can process what they are hearing. This is why repetition is so important. We have to say the same things often enough that they lodge within the listener's consciousness.

The tone the sermon takes is also important to its flow. Part of sermon assembly is determining the feel or tone that the sermon will demand. Anticipating where the sermon will need intensity and where it might settle for a more reflective pace will help the preacher think about what needs to be said as well as how it ought to be said. Intending tone in the process of assembly will make it easier and more effective for the preacher to communicate in the most appropriate way when it comes to actually preaching the sermon.

Remember that listening is hard work. There is no end of things to distract us. The girl two rows over is pretty. That reminds me of the movie that we watched last night. Did you notice that the preacher's pants are too wide or too narrow or too long or . . . wait, what was that he said? Listeners are going to tune in and tune out with various levels of frequency, especially if preachers charge forward with a singular pace. We will talk more later about how to deliver with a sense of pace and flow, but for now it is enough to say that sermons need to go easy on the content so that the preacher has the chance

4. Eugene L. Lowry, *Doing Time in the Pulpit: The Relationship between Narrative and Preaching* (Nashville: Abingdon, 1985).

to shape it—to pause and to repeat. Too much stuff means that there is no opportunity for the artistry that makes the sermon memorable.

So let's decide, then, to work only the two points of intention and incarnation in our Romans sermon. The point about impression is not so well established by the text and could end up creating clutter. As we move toward conviction, we will need to take some time. We have some things to confess. We won't be able to move too quickly.

That we must work time in a sermon about time is an irony when it comes to our preaching of Isaiah 60. One problem I have with this sermon is that there are so many pieces I could use, particularly in the first move of the sermon. I think that the most engaging thing I could do would be to offer my own reflection on the passage of time—how it seems to speed up while I am on vacation and slow down when I am at work. People can relate to that, so I should spend my time there. I may still want to use the slave imagery because there is a nice correspondence to the captivity of the people of Israel. But then again, not everyone will have seen the movie, and it could take too much time to describe. Perhaps I will use it, but only briefly, and only as a way to connect to the experience of Israel.

These are the kinds of considerations that an effective preacher works with. Just because something is worth saying does not mean that it will be helpful to say it. Preaching is engaging God through his Word and by his Spirit. We need to create space for the Spirit to do that thing the Spirit does. All these things take time.

This is the work of sermon assembly. Perhaps it is not as challenging as putting together an automobile, but then the purpose of a car is reasonably straightforward. The purpose of a sermon is to carry a message that will transform the world. We ought to give some care to it.

We have dreamed of high-speed trains and flying cars, transporter rooms, and jetpacks. Is there anything cooler than a jetpack? They promised us jetpacks. I am still waiting for mine. Gravity is so confining. We dream of ways we could be propelled to a different dimension—an altered level. We long for heaven but are stuck on earth, subject to the rules of the road. Our cars are great, but they do not let us fly. Our jets are helpful, but they cannot take us into orbit. Our spaceships can't even take us to the next planet, much less take us to the heaven that was promised.

A sermon is a powerful vehicle, with greater capacity than we give it credit for. A great sermon can transform us. It is a vehicle for the message that we will see God's kingdom come. The sermon can take us there, and it will if we assemble it and deliver it so that the Word is heard. The sermon is our jetpack to the kingdom, so let's strap on and see where it will take us.

15

Master the Outcome

I live in the world of hydroelectricity. The abundance of water flow we enjoy makes for reliable sources of renewable energy. Some of the largest hydro-electric dams in the world are located here in the Pacific Northwest. I remember visiting the Bennett Dam in northern British Columbia when I was a child. Even now I am amazed by the thought that the electricity sufficient to power an entire region can be generated by the flow of water through the massive turbines arrayed within the dam.

The basic physics involved is fairly simple. A turbine is a mechanical assembly with angled blades fitted around a rotor. As wind or fluid flows through the assembly, the rotor turns. The angled blades allow the water to flow through the mechanism, which is why these dams are typically installed on rivers and natural waterways. If the blades were not angled, the water would not be able to flow, causing the system to seize. A similar effect is achieved by windmills, strategically placed in high-wind areas. As the wind blows, the blades of the mill also function as a turbine, causing the mill to turn, which generates the desired power.

Turbines are meant to turn. As long as the water flows or the wind blows, the rotors move and power is produced. Dams are built to scale. The larger the turbines, the greater the amount of power that is generated. Power is the point as we look for ways to increase the effect of our efforts in the world.

We all deal with the fact of our personal limitations. We can increase our capacity through education and experience, but our personal capabilities will be most effectively leveraged through the use of some external source of power. Electrical power allows us to work longer into the evening. It allows us the use of tools and machinery such as computers that exponentially increase our ability to think, process, and understand. Preachers will need more than this. Preachers, who are looking to encourage spiritual transformation, will need external spiritual power.

Think of the integrative model as a four-bladed homiletic turbine through which the wind of the Holy Spirit is blowing. As the wind moves across our story, theme, gospel, and mission, the rotor turns and our preaching is empowered. We do our part to discover the message and assemble the sermon, but something more is needed.

Master: The Third Stage of the Integrative Method

The third stage of the integrative preaching process is *mastery*. Our specific interest here is the sermon *outcome*. Our first task was to discover the message—that thing that God wanted done through this text to these people at this time. Having understood the message, our second move was to assemble the sermon—the vehicle that would allow for effective communication of the message. Our third task, now, is to master the outcome. The outcome is the transformative effect that God intends for this sermon and message.

It is important that we understand that our purpose is not solely to discover a biblical message or to construct a vehicle capable of carrying such a message. We need to drive this message further so that it is allowed to have its full effect. Given that we are talking about a spiritual effect, we are going to need the Spirit's power. We can do a great job building homiletic turbines, but until the wind of the Spirit blows, the turbine will not turn, and we will not have achieved God's intention.

Old-time preachers used to speak about unction—the power of the Spirit that would anoint the sermon like oil, allowing for the free and effective empowerment of the objectives of the Holy Spirit.[1] We don't use the word so much these days, but perhaps we should. We are speaking here of the great oxymoronic mystery of the divine and human nature of the preaching task. The transformative purposes of God are enacted as the work of the human preacher is empowered by the work of the Spirit such that the outcome is realized in an exponential manner. God has chosen to work through human

---

1. "Unction means the anointing of the Holy Spirit on a sermon so that something holy and powerful is added to the message that no preacher can generate, no matter how great his skills." Lee Eclov, "How Does Unction Function?," in *The Art and Craft of Biblical Preaching: A Comprehensive Resource for Today's Communicators*, ed. Haddon Robinson and Craig Brian Larson (Grand Rapids: Zondervan, 2005), 81.

instrumentation. He has created us. He has gifted us. He has called us. But even that is not enough. He also empowers us as we engage him and embrace the thing he wants to do within us and through us. The wind blows, the turbine turns, and the outcome of the sermon is achieved.

All of this requires intentional action—the intent of God and the purposeful action of the preacher. While we will make effort to pray and master every aspect of the preparation process, it is important that we make a purposeful effort toward the assimilation of the sermon and the Spirit's power. There are things we can do to ensure a more robust mastery of the sermon outcome. We can own, share, speak, and pray the sermon and the message. As we do these things, in no particular order, we will tune our blades to catch the Spirit's power, allowing us to master the outcome that God intends for this event.

1. Own the Message

We have to *own* the message for ourselves. We have noticed that preaching is about the communication of a message that God applies first to the preacher and then through the preacher. This means that preachers need to move beyond an academic understanding of the things they intend to preach.

Where does this message live in my personal experience? When in my life has this been a significant concern? How have I personally struggled with this thing that God is saying? How am I succeeding in seeing this through?

In order to engage these questions, we have to work the model all the way around to mission. We have to be able to see the vision for this message as it applies in life—my life as the preacher first, before I ever offer it to others. What does this message look like in the practice of my life? How can I recognize its application for myself? There might be something right now that I am going to have to do before I can get up and share this truth with others. This is a question of integrity. Until this thing has been actualized in my own experience, I cannot speak of it with credibility to others.

If I am going to preach my Isaiah sermon, I am going to have to confront my own impatience. What am I longing for? There may be some specific instance of impatience that I am currently dealing with. Or I may need to scroll back to find some past time and place where this was a more pressing concern for me. I can bring that past experience forward, refreshing it in my memory so that it becomes current again.

I have, for example, a long-standing concern for justice in the world. I hate injustice. Whenever I see someone mistreated or wrongly convicted, it pains me almost physically. When the righteous are hurt or the unrighteous are acquitted, I find myself longing for heaven. How long, Lord, do we have to wait to see accountability for those who work violence on our women and children? How long till we see the faithfulness of your people recognized on earth as it is in heaven? Taking some time to own this highly personal struggle will bring me to the place where I can be more convincing when I make the point that "God is urgent for his promise within the timing of his purpose."

This requires an actual investment of time in the process. You have to stew on these things. You have to live with them for a while if they are going to ring true when you stand up before your listeners. If I am going to preach my Romans sermon, I'm going to have to spend some time owning the fact of my reluctance to use my feet. This world needs the gospel. How will they hear it unless I use my feet? I am using first-person pronouns with intention. If preaching is feet first, we are talking about my feet. When was the last time that I used them?

I may actually have to use my feet before I can ever offer this message to anyone else. I may have to get up on my feet and put one foot in front of the other until I find myself present to someone who will benefit from hearing the truth that if they simply call on the name of the Lord, they will be saved.

This is about the assimilation of the sermon, about making it our own. Until we own the message, our investment will be marginal. People can sense this stuff—they can sniff it out. Whether we speak to this directly or whether we keep quiet, they will be able to tell the truth of it. If our sermons are not true to us in the deepest way, they will not be powerful for those who listen. If we want to see the outcome, we need to own it first.

2. Share the Message

We also ought to *share* the message and its intended sermon. We typically think of preaching as a solitary exercise, where the preacher goes into isolation to prepare something that can then be unveiled before the people in some form of perfection. This thinking probably overappreciates the calling of the preacher while underappreciating the value of the Christian community in the discovery of the message from God's Word.

One of the most powerful things a preacher can do is to involve others before the sermon is fully formed. It is good to sustain the sermon as wet cement for as long as possible. That way the preacher can benefit from the insights and reactions offered by others, if they are allowed into the process. Public preaching is a communal enterprise, and so it is appropriate to bring the community into the process early on. For those whom we involve, the sermon we eventually present will dig deeper and ring truer. We have served our collaborators even as they helped us serve others more effectively.

Preachers have found various ways to do this kind of sharing. Some preachers gather in peer groups once a month to share and work the texts and topics they are developing. This approach usually does not offer deep reflection on each pastor's sermon, but it is a highly encouraging relational process that offers a venue for preachers to seek advice and describe stall points with others who understand the task of preaching.

Some preachers like to bring their sermons to the church staff, particularly to those involved in leading worship, for reflection and interaction prior to the preaching of it. These feedback opportunities become something like a dry run for the preacher, deepening the sermon within the preacher's consciousness, while allowing for helpful testing of the sermon and a more integrated worship plan.

Other preachers like to gather focus groups from the congregation for similar kinds of feedback. In these settings, preachers can test concepts to see how they will be heard by listeners in order to discern the most effective way to communicate various ideas. This can build confidence in the preacher for the live presentation.

One of my favorite ways to share before preaching is to run the sermon past my wife. In my early days I would preach the sermon into a tape recorder, prepare a list of questions, and then give it all to Karen for her response. These days we just talk about it over dinner, or while we are out walking in the evening. This has been helpful, both for my preaching and also for our marriage.

I actually did this sort of thing with my daughter prior to my preaching of the Isaiah sermon. Talking through the concepts of the sermon not only gave me more confidence in the preaching of it, but it allowed for some powerful teachable moments in my relationship with my daughter. She was struggling with the issue of time, as she was in that in-between time between engagement and marriage. Talking to her allowed me fresh insight into the sermon I was going to offer. I believe it helped me share the sermon with a greater credibility, even though I did not directly speak of her specific issue when I offered the sermon to the public.

My Romans sermon actually developed out of my teaching of the text in my seminary preaching class. We had talked through the text in some detail, which encouraged me to go ahead and prepare a sermon from the text. I then came back and shared that sermon with the students. This preparatory interaction empowered the sermon further, making it far more effective when I took it to the congregation.

Once we come to the conclusion that preaching is what God does—that we are just those who lead in listening—it becomes easier to share before the sermon has been perfected. We do not have to protect ourselves from any sense of shame that could attend to our thinking that the sermon is not yet a good representation of what we are capable of. This is not about us as individuals. This is about all of us together. We need to share these things.

3. Speak the Sermon

Another way to master the outcome is to *speak* the sermon into being. Preaching is oral communication. It is composed of words that must be spoken out loud. It helps if the public presentation is not the first time that we have offered those words with spoken voice. A vocal rehearsal of the material will help us find our voice and sense the substance of the sermon.

The audible voice is a powerful thing. Speaking our sermons will have a different effect from merely reading them in the quietness of our minds. Vocalizing our preaching, even in private, allows us to hear the sermon almost as if we were a listener ourselves, which of course we are. This practice allows us to step out of ourselves enough to hear our work from a different perspective. I am consistently surprised by the insights that derive from simply speaking my sermons out loud to myself. I learn things about my intentions that I could not otherwise perceive.

A second benefit to speaking the sermon into being is that it shapes the final product for oral delivery. There is something profoundly different about writing than speaking.[2] Writing is a tighter form of communication. A written product will be read and studied with care over time. Oral communication is heard and not read. It passes quickly in time, being erased immediately as it is spoken. It is more Snapchat than Instagram. Once words are spoken, they are hard to retrieve unless someone grabs them out of the air and commits them to writing. This is not to say that oral presentation is less valuable. Oral expression allows for a nuancing that written expression can only dream of. We have, for example, invented a whole new language known as emoji, a kind of hieroglyphics for contemporary textual communication. We know that humans have ways of communicating that mere writing cannot convey. It is in these things that orality excels. I have read the words of famous speeches,

2. "We—readers of books such as this—are so literate that it is very difficult for us to conceive of an oral universe of communication or thought except as a variant of a literate universe." Walter J. Ong, *Orality and Literacy: The Technologizing of the Word* (London: Routledge, 1982), 2.

but it would have been more powerful to have been present to hear Abraham Lincoln at Gettysburg or Martin Luther at the Diet of Worms.

Preaching, as oral communication, is powerful because it is so human. It presents ideas in a way that gets inside of us, because words and phrases are nuanced by a human speaker physically present to us. We are encouraged and exhorted and empowered. We do not need punctuation. The preacher punctuates the sermon by the manner of the preaching. If the sermon is published, as sometimes happens later on, it becomes a different kind of product, still useful, but useful in a different way. Given that preaching is going to be spoken, it makes sense that we speak it into being. If the product is going to be oral, perhaps the production ought to also take that form.

Personally, I like to go on walks—long walks where the sermon finds its shape and nuance in my consciousness. The message is already well established. The sermon has already been assembled. Now I work to find the language that will make this sermon sing. I speak the sermon to myself, out loud. I test expressions and find ways to describe the things I have in mind. Sometimes I like so much what I have found that I commit it to memory or write some portion of it down, but not too often. Mostly I am just trying to deepen the sermon within myself, assimilating its truth and assuring myself that I know of what I am going to speak. I don't know what people think when they see me mumbling to myself along the way, but I am not concerned by this. I walk and talk, and the sermon finds its voice within me.

I have observed that if I know something, I can speak of it. I have little difficulty waxing eloquent on the never-ending difficulties of my beloved Vancouver Canucks. I can talk about my golf swing for a very long time. I do not need a set of notes to be able to discuss the joy of playing with my grandson. These are subjects that I know with a deep knowledge formed from long experience. If I know something, I can trust myself to speak.

I want to know my sermons to the same depth. I have noticed, for example, how preachers will often work closely from a set of notes until it comes time for them to tell a personal story. At that point they will move away from their notes and speak simply from a depth of personal memory. They will not need their notes to tell their story. I have noticed, at that point, that every listener is engaged. Heads have snapped to attention across the congregation. People engage when preachers speak from their reservoir of personal conviction. I want to know the totality of my sermons to this degree or something near to it.

I am not trying to memorize a manuscript by this process, as that could be fatal. I have seen too many preachers lose their train of thought as they struggle to recall a memorized construction. I am simply finding fluency, getting comfortable talking through the sermon structure, seeking its cadence, and finding the confidence that will allow me to stand and deliver it. If the sermon has been well assembled, and if I know that assembly well in my heart, I can trust myself to speak it in the moment of the sermon. This level of awareness will empower the outcome of the sermon.

4. Pray the Sermon

A fourth way of mastering the outcome is to *pray* the sermon through. This is another hallmark of my preparatory walking. As I walk, I am not only speaking to myself, but I am speaking to the Lord about the message he is offering. This is a prayerful walking in the presence of God. If I am going to lead in listening, I need first to have listened to the Lord myself. This is significant to this stage of preparation.

I find this sort of praying to be particularly helpful immediately prior to the event of my preaching. I have found, for example, that Sunday morning is not a good time to be engaged in sermon crafting. The sermon ought to be assembled and assimilated long before I get to the hour before preaching. At this final point of preparation, I want to be in communion with the Father. I need to be in worship.

I have found it helpful in these moments to make the substance of the sermon the substance of my prayer. I will literally pray through the content of my sermon, bringing each piece to God. If I am going to speak about my grandfathers as a way of engaging people to hear the text in Romans 10, I will thank the Lord for the influence they had on me and my family generally. I will pray through my reluctance to use my own feet and reflect before the Lord on the fact that I will need to use my feet to preach this very sermon. Before preaching my Isaiah sermon, I will pray through my own longing to be present with the Lord, and the frustration of my own waiting. If there is a story about my wife, I will pray for my wife. If there is a metaphor from life, I will make that life circumstance the subject of my prayer.

This form of praying is effective in deepening the sermon within my consciousness, but more profoundly, it is a way of deepening my engagement with the God who is the preacher of this sermon. It is my job to lead in listening, and it is this prayer that ensures that I have done so.

Clock Time and Calendar Time

By these practices the sermon outcome is empowered. To the degree that we own, share, speak, and pray the sermon and its message, we can have confidence that the outcome God intends will be activated in the world.

All of this takes time—clock time and calendar time. My students often ask me how much time they should be prepared to spend in sermon preparation. They are always referring to clock time, the number of hours that they will need to spend to integrate their sermons. This is generally the wrong question. I have found that if the integrative model is well understood, a sermon can be prepared in relatively short order, if required. Sometimes a person only has a few minutes to prepare. The more time we have, the more effective we can be. I will generally take between eight and twelve hours to prepare a decent sermon. But it is less about clock time than calendar time. I will take what hours I can get, but I find that duration matters almost as much as quantity. Calendar time, or the span of time committed to preparation, is an underappreciated value.

Great preaching needs to gestate over substantial periods of time. It can take days or even weeks for a sermon to come to its maturity. I like to think of cooking preaching in a slow cooker.[3] It is a process of slow-cooking over time that allows the sermonic flavors to deepen and mature. This is a challenge, given that a lot of us are preaching every week. Sometimes a week is not enough for a sermon to fully find its flavor. For that reason, I like to work on multiple sermons simultaneously. In any given week, I might work on discovery for one sermon, assembly for another, and mastery and delivery for a third. That allows me two to three weeks of calendar time for every sermon, without a corresponding increase in clock time. It also allows for the sermons to flavor one another, like a good and tasty stew. This practice does not cost me anything in time, but it allows for a longer period of formation for my sermons. I am always encouraged when an important insight emerges in the latter stages of the process. Increasing calendar time gives me the space I need to fully integrate.

Our intentional efforts to master the sermonic outcome is about putting ourselves in the path of the Holy Spirit. Sometimes the power of the Spirit feels like the oozing of oil that slowly spreads. Other times it feels like a crashing cataract. But whenever we connect to the power of the Spirit, God uses us in a way we could not have imagined.

The Bennett Dam is not a natural wonder of the world. It was created by intention by human beings who put the materials in place. Yet the outcome of this emplacement is a natural result. The God-created, physical nature of the world has been harnessed for a focused outcome. The water God created and the force of its flow have been directed by humans, themselves created and

3. Kenton C. Anderson, "Slow-Cooking Your Sermons," *Leadership* 23, no. 1 (Winter 2002): 70.

endowed by God. The harnessing by humans of these physical phenomena does some credit to the people who put these things together. It offers even greater credit to the God who established the physics to begin with and who empowered these humans to think and know and understand how the water's flow could be used to greater benefit.

In this, the divine and human nature of our preaching is demystified. Our humanness is not a detriment when we consider that God created us. It was God who created, called, and gifted me to begin with. Any capacity I have was first endowed by him. As I learn to use and master my gifts, he picks them up and empowers them for greater outcomes than I could have imagined. This is what I live for. It is why I was created.

16

Deliver the Event

Karl Malone, former power forward for basketball's Utah Jazz, was known as "The Mailman" because he "always delivered." What that meant was that whenever his skills were needed, the team could count on Malone to provide what was required—he would make the shot, or set the pick, or make the defensive stop. He was reliable, which is another way of saying that he delivered.

Effective delivery is a fundamental human challenge. When I have something that we have agreed that you should have, I need to deliver that thing to you. It could be a product, a service, or even an idea, but whatever it is, I need to get it into your hands or into your mind in a reliable and efficient manner. This delivery must be timely so that you have it when you need it. It must be secure so that the thing arrives whole and undamaged. The delivery has to be reliable so that you can plan when to use it. Guaranteed delivery is critical to our ability to commit to our projects and concepts.

Historically, we have called this "shipping," because the original form of mass delivery was by ship—great sea vessels that would carry tea from India or silk from China. Motorization allowed for shipping across land by means of trains, trucks, and eventually airplanes. Container shipping has standardized delivery of mass amounts of goods and products. Zeppelins are now being used to deliver massive, heavy machinery to northern oil fields. Drones are being developed by Amazon to deliver packages more quickly and reliably. We have come a long way from the days of the Pony Express, though the basic task has remained unchanged—to transfer valued items across a distance from one person to another.

Deliver: The Fourth Stage of the Integrative Method

The fourth stage in the process of integrative preaching is *delivery*. At the end of the process, one person has to stand and deliver the message God intends by the vehicle of a sermon, empowered by the Spirit, for the benefit of all who listen. The preacher has to deliver, by which we mean the preacher has to present the message in a secure, reliable, and timely manner, such that the outcome of the sermon is assured. The message will transform us, if it can be delivered.

The preacher acts somewhat like a package deliverer who brings a message to another—though there is a crucial difference. When a person from FedEx or UPS delivers a package to a client, they leave upon completion of delivery. Their name is not given on the package. They have little idea as to what is inside, and they will not be around to witness its opening. They are satisfied that the package has found its intended destination. At that point, their job is done.

The preacher has a similar concern to see the package delivered, but with one important caveat. We have seen how preaching is an act of leadership—of leading in listening. The preacher is in fact the first listener, who, having taken delivery of the message, now shares that message with others. The preacher's name is on the package too. Upon delivery, the preacher acts as one of the recipients and will stand with those who receive. The preacher will even help the receivers to open the package, taking equal delight in what is found inside. This message is for the preacher too, who not only delivers but also receives along with all those others who have heard.

If the product of discovery is the message, and the product of assembly is the sermon, and the product of mastery is the outcome, the product of delivery is the *event*. To say that sermon delivery is an event is to say that something is happening here. Something tangible is going to happen. Preaching is not practiced in the abstract. Preaching happens in a place and time among a people God is calling. This is an event in God's presence.

To say that preaching is an event is to say that preaching is more than what can be published. It is true that we publish sermons and bind them into books. We upload sermons to websites and load them into cloud-based servers. In so doing, we establish sermons as products or as pieces that can exist in isolation, whether or not they are ever read or heard. But this is less than what we mean by preaching, which is why we understand the sermon as something other than its preaching.

To preach a sermon is to understand the relational aspect of the communicational process. We have a God who is speaking to those he has created.

Speaking is a living action that exists within a moment. It should not be abstracted and preserved under museum-quality glass. Preaching happens as God engages people by his Word and by his Spirit through the person of the preacher, who leads us all in our response.

Some of us will scoff, and some of us will sleep, and some of us will smile. Some will cringe, some will cry, and others will come and bow before the cross of Christ. Some will get angry. Some will be repentant. Some will be reluctant. Some will be indignant. Some will be indifferent. But something will happen because God is speaking, and when God speaks, we have to contend with what he says.

"In the presence of God," Paul told Timothy, we must "preach the Word" (2 Tim. 4:1–2). As those present to God, we deliver what we hear him saying, and it will change us in the moment of its hearing. It will transform us in our body, and it will change us in our soul. This is not a mere idea. This is an event. It cannot be repeated. It cannot be published. The words used can be published, but every time they are read or heard again, it will become a new event in God's presence because God speaks in time, and time is in motion. God is moving toward his purpose across time, and preaching is a means he uses.

To preach in God's presence also means the sermon must be spoken in the present. It is true that God has spoken and that he has worked to speak to people in the past. But this event is active in this moment. We need to speak as if the sermon is happening and not as if it happened in some other past time. We need to learn to speak in present tense so that the listener senses that the sermon lives. We need to describe problems and paint pictures that come across as vital and not as existing in some past reality. The truth is that God is alive and active, and so is his Word. The preaching of the living and active Word must affect the lives of those who listen, in keeping with the nature of the sermon as event.

Context and Tone

To speak of preaching as an event suggests that *context* matters. If the message that we preach describes what God is saying through this text to these people in this time, we are going to have to locate the event in the context of certain people in a particular moment in time. We must consider who these people are, as well as where and how they have gathered and to what purpose.

If the people have gathered for the express purpose of hearing from God and seeking him in worship, then the task is well understood, and the preacher can press forward with full confidence. If the listeners have not spoken of such purpose, then delivery will be more complex. The preacher will have to be more tactful, respecting the listeners' dignity, while still completing the delivery—a little like serving a subpoena, though for a more productive purpose. If the context is large, the dynamic will differ from that in a smaller one. If the context is formal, expectations will differ from those in a more casual situation. All of these are factors that will help to calibrate the approach the preacher will need to take in terms of tone, style, and presentation.

The best preachers are able to adapt to a variety of contexts. Preachers sometimes have it the other way around, believing that the people need to adapt to them—their preferences and their interests. But the preacher is the servant of the listeners. Great preachers are able to shape the message so that it can be heard and appreciated by listeners in their particular context. This is like what a missionary does when she or he adopts a different language and a different form of dress. The preacher learns to speak the language of the context, translating the truth of the message into a form that can be understood.

Some contexts and cultures are more structured in their expectations, and others less so. This often corresponds to the size of the gathering in which the sermon will be spoken. Larger groups will require a more structured and formalized presentation. Smaller groups will be looking for more personalized and responsive forms of communication. A great preacher will learn to be adept at both.

Tone

One aspect requiring calibration is the sermon tone. Tone refers to a number of issues such as volume, pace, and intensity, but primarily it is about the nature of the communication relationship. Will this context require a more monological or dialogical approach? Would this event best be served by a more precise and formal presentation style, or would a more informal, casual approach be better suited to the need?

As we have seen, this question is all about contextual considerations. Larger settings typically require more structured presentations. They will likely require a more monological tone. Smaller crowds, by contrast, typically allow for a greater sense of dialogue and spontaneity. Larger crowds tend to respond to a precise and focused discourse, while smaller crowds will allow for a more open, fluid dynamic. Of course, some cultures are more formal even in smaller settings, and others allow for greater freedom even in larger gatherings. The preacher has to do some cultural anthropology to discern what will be most helpful.

Our tone may depend on the sense of import that attaches to a specific moment. It could be that a congregation has a normal pattern of less structured presentation, but certain moments may require a greater sense of occasion. A special anniversary, a funeral, or a moment of crisis each could demand a different tone. The preacher will need to learn to read these situations to discern the tone that is appropriate.

There is no one right way for any of this, which is why the preacher needs to be capable of leaning in either direction. It is a useful rule of thumb to affirm that preaching ought to be as relational and dialogical as can be managed within the strictures offered by the moment. Leaning toward the relational will maximize engagement, which is always helpful, even if the preacher is the only one who is physically speaking, which is often the case with standard sermons.

The monological nature of most preaching can still offer a dialogical feel when practiced well. The preacher can use rhetorical questions, can pause more, and can be more intentional about anticipating listeners' thinking even if no one else is saying anything out loud. A skillful preacher will help the listeners to feel they are part of a conversation, even in a formally presented sermon.

I remember recording a radio program some years ago. The producer challenged me to speak as if I were talking to a single person just across the table and not to think about the fact that there were thousands listening. Speaking to the one will always serve as proxy for the many. Sometimes we might even want to do this literally, speaking directly to a single trusted member of the crowd. As you connect with the one, the many will likewise feel connected.

Appearance

Our personal appearance is another way by which we communicate. How we dress is another form of human language. Dress communicates more than what we sometimes imagine. The problem is that these things are culturally determined. A tie might be mandatory in some places. In other places they might want to hang you with it. In some contexts, casual dress is the norm. In some of these places, they have unwittingly created a new formality. It might look casual, but it is the expected uniform. It would be perilous to deny the expectation.

I think it generally wise for the preacher to be dressed somewhere within the top thirtieth percentile of the congregation in terms of formality. In other words, if 30 percent of the people in the congregation are wearing suit jackets or sport coats, it would be wise for the preacher to be at that level also. To go beyond that, perhaps with a crisp white shirt and tie, might be seen as ostentatious. You want to be one of the better-dressed people in the crowd, without being so well dressed that you are making folks uncomfortable. You are a leader, and your manner of dress is one of the ways that you create a tone of confidence among the people for the leadership you offer through your preaching.

Overall, the tone must convey that the message matters. It has to matter to the preacher before it will matter to the listeners, and the listeners will be astute to know how much the preacher cares. Listeners will know whether the preacher is going through the motions. They will be able to tell by whether the preacher adds intensity where intensity is warranted and a more reflective tone where that makes sense. The preacher is not merely saying words but expressing them, like a great singer who can engage the audience through his or her passion.

Tone can sometimes be manipulated, but typically listeners will sniff out any lack of authenticity. The tone will match what is in the preacher's heart. This means that the best way to manage tone is for the preacher to truly care and to be present to the people in this moment. We preach in the presence of God. That is the context for this event. A tone authentic to the context will always have a stronger chance of being heard with appreciation.

The Sermon Script

The sermon script is another matter that depends on context. Preachers can choose to work from a complete manuscript, to speak extemporaneously, or to work from some kind of partial, hybrid script. How a sermon manuscript is built will have a significant effect on the preaching that results.

Typically, full manuscripts result in a more precise and more formal presentation. This is in the nature of writing. While it is possible to speak a sermon into writing, expressing content orally, before committing it to paper, the very process of forming sentences and paragraphs will conspire to create a more literate and less oral form of presentation. That said, a manuscript can be helpful in disciplining sermon content, focusing thought and sharpening expression. Working completely without notes can lead to an undisciplined and less thoughtful final product.

In general, I think an oral form of composition is in order. Sermons were meant to be spoken, not read. People's literacy levels are usually overestimated.[1]

1. Grant Lovejoy, "'But I Did Such *Good* Exposition': Literate Preachers Confront Orality" (paper presented to the Evangelical Homiletics Society, October 2001).

Orality is a different way of being than is literacy.[2] Literate work requires a sense of polish that is not natural in regular interpersonal discourse. Oral work is more poorly punctuated. It doesn't follow the grammar that your eighth-grade teacher taught you. Oral speech is more repetitious. Its sentences are shorter. Sometimes the sentences overlap or trail off incompletely. Take, for example, one of your recent conversations on a subject that you and your partner deeply cared about. Can you imagine a transcript of that dialogue? I suspect that it would be a mess. Normal communication is not terribly polite and careful in its composition. It is looser, more animated, and it works. We seldom leave a conversation without a sense that we have been heard.

The best way to compose a sermon, then, is to take a well-assembled structure and then speak it into being.[3] You are not going to read this to the people. This is going to be spoken to them audibly, which means that an orally composed script will be the most likely way to end up with something that the people will be able to hear.

Still, I understand the laziness that can attend to this. Some of us, blessed with the gift of gab, will be tempted to shortcut our preparation. We will take this encouragement to orality as a license to wing it. It will seem faster and easier, and under the pressure of any given moment in ministry, we will take what seems the easy way and feel justified in doing it.

In actual fact, an oral script is not an easy route. It could actually take more time to properly master the sermon and its outcomes. My best suggestion is to adopt a hybrid approach to the subject—what I call the "summary manuscript." Invest deeply in discovery and assembly. Make sure the sermon is well and properly built and mastered by all the means available. Then take that sermon and speak its content into being. Develop it orally so that it feels like something that was made to be spoken. Then record the sermon in summary form, something between five hundred and a thousand words. That will not be enough to be spoken in public. Most sermons when presented will need to be two or three times that length. But it is enough to make sure that the sermon finds a focus. Take that summary manuscript and make sure that you deeply own it. You don't have to memorize it, but you do need to know it. Pray it through. Share it with others. Talk it through, out loud, until you are comfortable expressing it. Again, don't memorize this. You are not planning to recite the summary. You are going to preach

---

2. Walter J. Ong, *Orality and Literacy: The Technologizing of the Word* (London: Routledge, 1982).

3. See Charles W. Koller, *Expository Preaching without Notes* (Grand Rapids: Baker, 1962), and Dave McClellan, *Preaching by Ear: Speaking God's Truth from the Inside Out* (Wooster, OH: Weaver, 2014).

the sermon that has been orally developed and empowered through a deep assimilation.

This is a skill that may require development. It may be more important in the early stages of one's development to have a more complete set of notes. This is not a matter for dogmatism. This is a practical question as to what will be most helpful in your context.

The Physical Tools

In addition to the script, there are other tools you might consider. Are you going to use a pulpit, or are you going to sit on a stool? Will you use a slide presentation? What about props and other physical objects? Is it better to stand above the congregation on a platform or to come down and stand among the people? These are questions without clear answers but with significant consequences. There is no correct way to discern these things, although what we do determine will have calculated implications. Again, it is about understanding the context and how communication works within the setting of your preaching.

Take the pulpit, for example. Yes, please, take it. It is getting in the way. Unless, of course, your context views the pulpit as a symbol of the centrality of the preached Word and, were you to remove it, you might be putting your safety, or at least your employment, in jeopardy. There are times when the pulpit must be taken seriously for what it represents, but most of the time it is simply there to hold your notes. But what if we do not have any notes? The pulpit might just then be in the way. At the very least, we could reduce it to a music stand, but then that tends to look a little weak.

An objection to preaching without some kind of pulpit or podium is that it puts the preacher front and center. Too much attention on the person of the preacher can erode attention on the message from the Word. But perhaps that too is a matter of one's tone and general presentation. I believe that it is possible to stand in front of a crowd of people, look them in the eye, and speak with honesty and integrity the message that God has given from his Word. The less stuff we have in the way, the more effectively we will communicate.

Props and objects are another case in point. Will the use of these visual aids be helpful or harmful in the communication of the message? A prop is a visual metaphor. It allows us to support what we are saying with what the people are seeing. We can work the prop with our hands, according to its purpose, allowing the listener a stickier, more persistent experience. This is positive. If we are going to paint pictures in our preaching, a prop is just a more tangible and physical expression of such. This should be helpful, unless it is poorly done. Props suffer the same potential pitfalls as worded illustrations. They can be misfit, leading listeners in unintended directions. They can distract. They can be fumbled. That said, there is nothing fundamentally wrong with using visual objects and plenty right about the practice, so long as they are handled well and to good purpose.

One could say something similar about projected slides. The development of affordable overhead projection units has been a great thing for the church. It has allowed us to sing more current music and to utilize video and to use imagery in preaching and in worship. But as with everything else, it has to be done well to be effective. Projected imagery has an amplifying effect similar to our microphones and sound systems. With these technologies, whatever we say or do is writ large and multiplied. Our voices are louder, our images are bigger, and our mistakes are more obvious. It puts a little extra pressure on us to be great, especially when people are so accustomed to excellence in media production. Unless we can afford professional digital tools or can employ people with this expertise, we risk playing to our weaknesses instead of our strengths. Most of us will not be able to produce media to the standard expected in the broader culture. The good news is we do not need to.

The strongest image is that of an authentic human being standing in front of others in the flesh to share a message that they value. There is not a video in the world that can top that. We do not need to distract people away from our personal expression by poorly produced digital media.

A common mistake that preachers make with PowerPoint is to fill the screen with words. Not only is this dull, but it is unattractive. We could, on the other hand, project more pretty pictures. But it can be extremely difficult to find an appropriate image that nails the concept you are going for. It may be that you are working through some complex material and that it is helpful to lay out a chart or some text that helps people see what you are saying more clearly and memorably. It may also be helpful to project a picture of something that you are talking about. But perhaps it would be helpful, after having clarified things by your imagery, to turn the screen off until it is needed once again. There is no requirement to have the screen going for your whole sermon. If you don't, it will have more impact when you do.

As to video, my counsel is to be careful. Video is a very different media from oral proclamation. It has a different approach and occupies a different mental state. Interrupting the flow of one's preaching to show a video clip is almost always a poor idea. It can be very difficult to get attention focused back on you and on your sermon. If the video is clipped from a professionally produced motion picture, the effect on consciousness will be jarring. These videos can be helpful as a lead-in to the sermon, providing that they are not too long. They can also be productive as a wrap-up piece. But they are almost never helpful in the context of the sermon's flow. If, as has been said, a picture is worth a thousand words, who knows how many words a video might represent? Make sure those words are the right ones and that what you are presenting drives the things that you intend and not some mental distraction.

One more thing should be said about our mental attitude. Fear is a natural consequence that attends to the public nature of our preaching. Preparing to preach is fine. Standing to preach is a fearful prospect. It is in this final stage that we find ourselves most vulnerable, accountable for the things we have prepared ourselves to say. It can be frightening.

It is important, when battling fear, to understand what we are afraid of. Is it the people? Is it our own sense of inadequacy? Are we concerned that we will be exposed as something less than what we aspire to? Are we afraid that God himself might be disappointed by the sermon we offer for his Word?

It could be any or all of these things. Things are at stake whenever we stand and preach. If our fear is focused on ourselves, on our vulnerability—what we lack and how people might despise us—we have lost the purpose of our preaching, and our fear will cripple us. This is the fear of man.

The fear of God is more productive. To fear God as preachers is to be mindful of our limitation and the weakness of our offering. It is to recognize that we do not speak as God but for God, and only as God chooses to bless and honor with his power. To fear God is to be aware of the things that are at stake for people, for the church, and for the kingdom and its coming on earth as it is in heaven. To fear God is to respect and worship him as the reason, the substance, the motivation, and the power of our preaching.

In the end, it is God who delivers. It is his Word, and it is his purpose. He is the surety that the message will find its home. All of our technologies are designed to help us overcome the distance of geography and psychology that keeps us separated from each other and from the truth. Our ships and trucks and planes and drones—even our pulpits and projectors—are constructed to help us deliver value to each other, when God has already brought us everything we truly need. God has delivered his Word to us in Christ. It is our joy as preachers to pass along what was first delivered to us by God.

CONCLUSION

In conclusion, let me tell you a story. On October 10, 1707, a fleet of British naval vessels left Gibraltar to return home to England. Led by celebrated admiral Sir Cloudesley Shovell, those aboard were anticipating an uneventful return.[1] Instead, more than fourteen hundred of these sailors lost their lives in one of the greatest maritime tragedies in the vaunted history of the British navy. After miscalculating their position, the fleet struck rocks near the Isles of Scilly, and four ships were lost. This misfortune could have been avoided if there had been a way for them to know their nautical position.

The difficulty was an inability to determine longitude. Latitude was relatively easy to locate, as one only had to plot one's position relative to the sun at its highest point in the sky. There was no such fixed point of reference, however, for the determination of longitude. The problem was not Shovell's alone. The problem of longitude was so intractable that the British Parliament established a prize of twenty thousand pounds (a ridiculously large sum of money at the time) to be awarded to anyone who could discover a reliable method for determining an accurate measurement of longitude at sea. It was several decades before the prize would be awarded. In the meantime, thousands of lives and untold millions in goods and services were wasted.

Some of the proposals for solving longitude were comical. Mathematicians William Whiston and Humphrey Ditton thought that producing audible reference points across the ocean could solve the problem. The plan was to anchor ships at various intervals across the sea from which cannons would be fired at fixed times. Sailors could then judge their position by the sound.

1. Dava Sobel, *Longitude: The True Story of a Lone Genius Who Solved the Greatest Scientific Problem of His Time* (London: Walker, 1995).

Sir Kenelm Digby proposed using the "powder of sympathy," which was supposed to cure wounds by application to the cause of the injury instead of to the wound itself. Digby's theory was that a wounded dog could be put aboard a ship, with the animal's bandage left in the trust of a timekeeper back in London. The timekeeper would dip the bandage into the powder at noon Greenwich time each day, causing the creature to yelp. This would give the ship's captain an accurate knowledge of the time, from which he could judge the longitude.

A seemingly more scientific, though just as implausible, solution was proposed by John Flamsteed, the Astronomer Royal, who attempted to create an exhaustive map of the stars of the heavens, from which mariners could more accurately fix their position. Flamsteed worked on the project for forty years, never completing this impossible task.

Eventually the problem was solved by John Harrison. His solution was to create a clock that could tell the time at sea. Once the captain knew the time, figuring out the longitude was a simple calculation. Harrison's achievement was more difficult than what you might imagine given the potential for the warping and rusting of the materials most often relied on for clock making. It took several years for the Board of Longitude to confirm the accomplishment and to award him the prize.

Today we take global positioning for granted, but even in our time we need more than one coordinate. With reference to our integrative model, we might be able to sort ourselves out along the horizontal line. It doesn't require theology to physically integrate the head with the heart. But if we want to find the longitude, the vertical line that brings heaven to the human, we are going to need a different kind of solution.

Harrison's clock was difficult to credit. It was almost as if it were too easy. One simply looked at the clock, compared it to the charts, and the problem was solved. It was as if the problem were addressed by revelation.

Our attempts to resolve our own issues—to locate our purpose in the world apart from the revelation of God—are about as useful as Whiston and Ditton's cannons or Digby's powder. We must have both coordinates—latitude and longitude, the physical and the spiritual—and we will not have them until we can read the clock, until we hear from God, who speaks to us objectively.

There is, perhaps, no better news than that the God who created us continues to care for us—that he has forgiven us in Christ and has an ongoing purpose for us, which he is pleased to reveal to us through his Word, by his Spirit, and through those of us who stand and preach. Though we have the privilege to share in this, we do not claim much for ourselves. This is his project. It is a top-down enterprise, as it is always God who takes the initiative. It is God himself who speaks.

So stand somewhere and preach the Word. Engage people. Instruct them. Lead them to conviction and send them out on mission. Set your sermon into motion so that the coil torques around the center point of the cross. As you do, his kingdom will come, on earth as it is in heaven.

Appendix

Sermon Examples

Earlier in this book I spoke of how preaching is an oral enterprise—that it is spoken into being and not written. I spoke of how preaching is offered by preachers, human beings who are able to show the nuances and the punctuation marks simply by the manner of their communication. This is what makes preaching powerful. It is the physical presentation of truth in a given moment.

I stand by all of that. Yet the challenge of this book is to help preachers understand how to carry out this preaching, and so, it seems, examples are in order. Throughout the latter chapters of the book, I utilized two examples, one from the Old Testament (Isa. 60) and one from the New Testament (Rom. 10). I thought it would be helpful to show the sermons in manuscript form, as I have done below.

These sermons are offered for the purpose of analysis, though that was never the intention for these sermons. In fact, they have never been presented publicly in the exact form you see below. They were developed and preached orally in the manner I have described throughout the book. I wrote these manuscripts after the fact, from my memory of the events. I am certain that the actual sermons were fuller and more effective than what you will see here. Take them for what they are. They are not transcripts, but they are reasonable facsimiles of the sermons as presented.

As mentioned earlier, I do not consider these to be pinnacle examples of the very best in preaching. If we were to wait for me to produce something perfect, this book would never be completed. These are sermons that I delivered in the practice of my ministry. I thought them reasonable examples of the integrative method. Perhaps they will be helpful.

The Purpose of Time: Isaiah 60:22

God is urgent for his promise within the timing of his purpose.

There is a freshness about this time of year. The month of January brings a sense of newness—like a crisp blanket of snow or a clean sheet of paper. The whole year lies in front of us with all of its opportunity. Time is promising.

I find myself thinking a lot about time this time of year. Looking back and looking forward, I can never quite get my head around how time works. They say that time moves faster the older we get. It certainly seems to be the case. Why is it that while we are on vacation, time seems to move quickly, but that after we return from the holiday, the same period of time takes on a heightened sense of proportion in our memory—in effect, lengthening our sense of vacation? "Where is this present?" asked the psychologist William James. "It has melted in our grasp, fled ere we could touch it, gone in the instant of becoming."

There are theories about this. BBC broadcaster Claudia Hammond describes the "proportional theory" of time, which suggests a solution from the world of mathematics. A day occupies a larger proportion of a younger person's accumulated time than that of an older person, which may account for the sense that time moves faster the older we get. But this doesn't apply with any strict rationality, given that some days seem to pass slowly even for those of us who have reached a certain age. More accurately, Hammond suggests, our perception of time warps around the degree of vividness of an event, along with the number of times that we have recollected the event.

Time seems like it ought to be mechanical and mathematical. A century is composed of fixed and immutable numbers of decades, years, months, weeks, days, hours, minutes, and seconds. They are incessant in their march, accumulating regardless of the level of attention that we give them, raising anxiety in the person coming ever nearer to the certainty of their end—at least for us as individuals.

Tempus fugit—time flies when we're having fun, but not so much when we are otherwise burdened. Prisoners talk of "doing time," which suggests that time is something that has to be worked and worried. I recently saw the movie *12 Years a Slave*, which depicts the injustice experienced by Solomon Northrup and his fellow slaves. I watched them sing of their hope of Jordan and their sense that time would bring salvation, either in this world or in the next. This led me to reflect on the people of Israel held captive to the Babylonian nation, crying out for their delivery, languishing in slavery, wondering whether there would ever be a time when they would know God's promise. You can do the time when you can find the hope.

The promise holds that a redeemer will come. Isaiah 60 speaks of light that has come and glory that has risen. Nations return, and families are reunited. Hearts swell as joy appears. Walls are rebuilt. Wealth is spread. Oppressors submit as all who have been forsaken find everlasting pride and generational joy. Bronze is traded in for gold. Violence is a memory. The sun is no longer necessary, as God himself brings light forever. In captivity the people felt diminished. They felt small. But God says in verse 22, "The least of you will become a thousand, the smallest a mighty nation." For the people locked within the misery of captivity, this is a sustaining promise.

It is the timing of this promise that is in question. What the people experience as hope, Isaiah describes as fulfillment. The prophet writes *proleptically*, describing the future as if it has already happened. "*I am the LORD; in its time I will do this swiftly.*"

It is an oxymoron—a wise kind of foolishness that integrates a sense of urgency with a sense of patience. I will act swiftly, but not until the time is right. It is the suggestion that God can be relied on for his promise, but that there are larger purposes that must be attended to within the chronology of God's intent. It is to affirm that *God is urgent for his promise within the timing of his purpose.*

It helps us to observe that God exists outside time. This is to say that God is *eternal*. Once we appreciate how God has no beginning and no end, we can begin to appreciate the relativity of time from an eternal perspective. Einstein merely realized something of the mystery of a God for whom a day is like a thousand years and a thousand years are like a day.

But this is not to say that time has no purpose. God invented time. From his place outside time, God created the world within the regularity of time. Humans experience life one thing at a time, which suggests that there is a *trajectory* to time. Time is headed somewhere. We do not live our life on a Möbius strip—a Sisyphean experience of looped time that repeats without end and to no purpose. God is up to something. This is going somewhere. The existence of time implies the necessity of hope. Without hope—the sense that there is purpose for our days—the invention of time would be cruel, like the prisoner without hope of parole. But in God's economy, time attaches to eschatological purpose so that believers can have hope that life itself has purpose. It's all just a matter of time.

All this is seen in the person of Jesus himself, who came "in the fullness of time." There are two kinds of time described in the Bible—*chronos* time and *kairos* time. *Chronos* time is clock time—seconds and minutes and hours. *Kairos* time describes the opportune moment of indeterminate time when everything comes together. God has a plan for his purpose, and he will unfold things when the time is exactly right. If we were capable of pushing the timeline, we would miss the fulfillment of God's intention for the people we love and even for ourselves. We can trust that God is urgent for his promise but that this urgency exists within the timing of his purpose.

You will want to notice the verses that immediately follow in chapter 61. "The Spirit of the Sovereign LORD is on me, because the LORD has anointed me to proclaim good news to the poor." If this sounds familiar, it ought to. Jesus returns to his hometown, Nazareth, and makes his way into the synagogue. Standing up to read, someone hands him the scroll of Isaiah. Carefully he unrolls the scroll and begins to read these words laid out in chapter 61. "He has sent me to proclaim freedom for the prisoners and recovery of sight for the blind, to set the oppressed free, to proclaim the year of the Lord's favor." Solemnly, he rerolls the scroll, hands it back to the attendant, and takes his seat. Every eye is fixed on him. "Today," he says, "this scripture is fulfilled in your hearing."

It was time—God's time, *kairos* time. God had not forgotten his promise. Jesus came in the fullness of time, proving God's urgency for his promise within the *kairos* timing of his purpose. This was gospel timing, when the conditions were right for the Savior to appear.

Can you imagine being in that synagogue as the light began to dawn on you that this was more than just another prophet? Can you imagine standing at the empty tomb, just beginning to realize that God's promise was not empty?

What if you understand your own impatience in the context of his promise? I know that things are broken, that things frustrate. I know it feels like God forgets and fails to fulfill the promise you have counted on. I know it feels we've been forgotten while we scuffle on this planet that has itself forgotten God. But then, perhaps it is we who have forgotten that there is a time and season. It was a long time before the promise and Christ's coming—hundreds of years of pain and blindness. But Jesus came—in the fullness of time. When he came, he brought salvation so that our pain and struggle were no longer without purpose. God did not forget. In his time, God acted swiftly. He showed himself urgent for his promise, in the good timing of his purpose.

It is an oxymoron—an alchemy of disparate elements that unify to describe the way that heaven touches earth. I am not a patient person. I have a lot of trouble waiting. I put a lot of stock into God's promise. I have bet my life on the hope his word inspires. I am looking for a lot from God, and when he doesn't seem to move with the alacrity I expect, I can get a little frustrated. And when I let this frustration get the best of me, I can miss the purpose of God's promise. I begin to doubt the urgency of God. The benefits of hope are then lost to me.

Before Karen and I were married, she took a trip to England for a month with her best friend. This was difficult for me, because I was living in Calgary at the time—her city—and I didn't have my own family to lean on. I bought a calendar and put it up on my wall, drawing a big X through every day that passed. That month I was "doing" time. Time was something to be worked, and the work was hard and worrisome.

Just before she left, Karen blessed me with this picture. You can see that on it she painted the words of Proverbs 13:12: "Hope deferred makes the heart sick, but a longing fulfilled is a tree of life." I lived the truth of that, that month of August. When Karen returned, we were more happy to see each other than we had ever been, and a tree grew up that has given us life for more than thirty years.

God is urgent for his promise within the timing of his purpose. We don't always know his purpose. We don't always know the time. And so we wait. They that wait on the Lord, Isaiah says, renew their strength. And so we wait—and the waiting makes us stronger.

And so we wait—knowing that if we push the timeline, we may miss the blessing . . .

And so we wait—understanding that time is warped when measured by forever . . .

And so we wait—in faith that God wants more for us than we could want ourselves . . .

And so we wait—in hope that there is purpose in the waiting that only God might know.

"In its time, I will do this swiftly." Let me give you another oxymoron: patient longing, a kind of anticipatory contentment. It takes faith to live with patient longing. To long without patience is to live in desperation. To have patience without longing is to embrace the cynicism of the sovereign moment. It is to believe that there is safety in accepting that there is nothing more than now. It is not a Christian way to live. Patient longing—Christians live for the future in the context of the present. Christian faith allows believers to be content in the moment, in the knowledge that God has something better in his time. Faith does not measure by the limits of the moment. Faith expands the moment with the promise of God's future.

This is a good word. Whatever you know in the moment is not all that God has for you. God is on mission. His promises are eternal in their glory. No matter how discouraged you might feel because the circumstances conspire against you in the tyranny of the moment, you can let hope grow in the knowledge that God has something more in store and that when it comes, everything that has been paining you will seem a foggy memory.

When Karen came home from England, it was sweeter than it would have been if she had never been away. The waiting seemed interminable, and yet the return seemed somehow like the work of a moment. You know how that is, that the thing that seemed so long in coming arrives, it seems, in an instant—the troubles melted in our grasp, fled ere we could touch them, gone in the instant of becoming something bigger and grander in the timing of God's purpose.

And so we wait.

Preaching with Your Feet: Romans 10:13–15

Preaching is feet first.

They say you can tell a lot about a person by looking at their hands. Take my grandfathers, for example. I had two grandfathers. One was a mechanic and the other was a carpenter, and you could tell things about them just by looking at their hands.

Grandpa Warwick delighted in fixing things and making them work. He used to collect junk from the town dump, which he would turn into useful things. He once built a little car for my brother and me. It was powered by a lawn mower engine, and at a top speed of twelve miles per hour, it wasn't fast, but it was powerful. He put a rear-end differential into our little car so that we could turn around tight corners. I know he did this out of love for us, but I suspect he also did it just because he could. I would look at his hands, encrusted with deep layers of grease and grime. It would have taken a month of washings to get his hands to begin to give the appearance of clean. His hands spoke to me of effort and purpose and creativity.

Grandpa Volker was the carpenter. He built many of the homes around the town that I grew up in. I would see him come home in his blue construction van with the ladder hanging from the side and the tools and lumber arrayed inside. I remember examining his hands. They were scarred and blistered, with calluses and sometimes splinters. His large and capable hands showed me he was serious about his business. My grandfather built homes for families, and he did it at the expense of his own comfort.

Now to me. I have these small, uncalloused, unimpressive, preacher hands. Actually, I have one callus, just underneath my wedding band. I think it comes perhaps from gripping the steering wheel too tightly on the way to board meetings. It is a good thing for me that our text says that preachers are not judged by their hands. Preachers are judged by their feet. Preaching is feet first.

Preaching the gospel is expected of God's people. When we do it with our feet, the Lord sees it as something beautiful. This expression in Romans 10:15 was first expressed in Isaiah 52. God's people were in captivity, struggling to find the patience to await the Lord's deliverance. "My people have been taken away for nothing, and those who rule them mock" (v. 5). Yet the day will come for a deliverer. In that day, they will know that it is God himself who speaks (v. 6). One day, the people would look up from their captivity, and they would see their savior come down from on the mountain, and that will be a beautiful day. "How beautiful on the mountains are the feet of those who bring good news" (v. 7).

It is always a beautiful thing to hear good news, and there is no better news than of the promise of salvation. We are all captive in our various ways, confined by expectations and oppressions that subvert and fail the intention for which we each were created. We all struggle for what we have. We have all fallen short of God's glory. Our sin has seen to that.

But we have the promise that the Word of God is near us (Rom. 10:8). It is in our mouth and in our heart. All we need to do is own it—to confess that Jesus is Lord. If we believe in our heart that God has raised him from the dead, we will be saved (v. 10). In fact, everyone who calls on the name of the Lord will be saved (v. 13).

This is good news—the best news—if only it were known by those to whom the message has been intended. How can anyone call on one they have not believed in? How can they believe in one of whom they have not heard? How can they hear if there is no preacher? And who will preach unless someone is sent (v. 14)?

It is this sense of sending that requires the use of feet. This building up of questions suggests a sense of motion. It is a cascading flow of logic, intended to encourage us to go and speak so that people can hear and ultimately believe, but we will not go unless we use our feet.

Preaching with the feet has at least two implications. The first is that our preaching will be intentional. No one has ever used their feet by accident. Using one's feet is always the result of a determined intention of the will. When we woke up this morning, we needed to choose to swing our legs out from the comfort of our beds, to place our feet on the ground, and to stand up on them. It required a courageous act to put one foot in front of the other so that we were propelled toward the day's agenda. You have to choose to use your feet. They will not operate in any other way.

This is the implication of the Romans rhetoric. Belief is intentional. We have to choose to listen to our calling. We will not preach unless we decide to. We will not go unless we choose to use our feet. Preaching and believing are acts of intention, and when they are chosen, it is a thing of beauty.

The second implication of preaching feet first is that such preaching is incarnational. Whenever we use our feet, we are moved to some new place. The feet, more than any other bodily appendage, are the instruments of our propulsion. Feet take us places, which is why the connection between feet and sending in Romans 10 is so significant. Preaching requires sending because it requires presence. You cannot share the message without being present. You need to physically incarnate yourself in the presence of another if you are going to preach.

Perhaps this is why preaching is so unpopular on both sides of the transaction. Preachers hesitate to preach because it requires vulnerability. We need to be present to preach. We need to be within striking range, which means that we could be struck ourselves. Those who hear our preaching likewise are averse to such an accountability. Preaching from a distance is easily dismissed. Preachers who use their feet to become present must be contended with. Incarnational preaching must be accounted for.

Beautiful preaching is feet first.

I admit I have a hard time with this. This is not how I would have written the text myself. If you or I were to write this passage, we might feature an alternative body part. How beautiful is the tongue, perhaps. How beautiful the throat, the mouth, or the lips that bring good news—anything but the feet.

I would have preferred the tongue. I am pretty good with my tongue. I can speak, and speaking is safer, as far as I am concerned. I can communicate the gospel with my mouth and tongue, and I can keep my distance. Especially in these days, I can broadcast the message. I can tweet it or blog it, sending it out as digital content, and I might never have to use my feet. I can keep safe if I don't use my feet. I do not have to be physically present to offer the gospel.

This is true, and I am grateful for it. I am happy for the opportunities provided by technology, and I am grateful every time that God chooses to use these means to bring glory to himself and to bring the gospel to a new believer. But if this is the only way by which I share the message, then I have not truly been like Jesus.

Jesus used his feet. Jesus was the incarnate Son of God who came down from Mount Zion—who came down from the right hand of the Father in heaven and embodied himself in our presence so that we could know God physically and not just spiritually. This is an integrated knowledge of God that was possible only because Jesus was willing to use his feet. He allowed himself to be touched, sharing his life with us in the flesh, and it was a beautiful thing. Because Jesus came in feet and flesh, we were truly able to know him and to be forgiven by him. The preaching of Jesus was feet first. He came to us and among us so that we could know him. We loved him and listened to him until such time that some of us put nails into those beautiful feet.

I would have loved to have seen those feet. I would have liked to have seen Paul's feet—calloused and blistered, smelling and stinky, scarred and chafed and beautiful feet. Paul's feet took him everywhere in the world where there were people who needed to hear that if they would only believe in their heart and confess with their mouth that Jesus is Lord, they could be saved. They could be saved from their bondage to sin. They could be saved from the penalty that their rebellion demanded. They could be saved from the frustration and futility and impatience that their sorry lives described. They could be saved for all eternity if they would only believe and confess. The only way the people would know this was if Paul used his beautiful feet.

I wonder about my feet. I wonder about our feet—how beautiful they are. Do you remember when Jesus met with the disciples, just prior to his death? He ate with them, and he shared with them, and then he washed their feet. It was an act of generosity, a symbol of his servant heart. By washing their feet, he showed them that he loved them. They could then use those feet to likewise serve others.

Historically, churches like this at the close of sermons like this would call for people to get up onto their feet and to use those feet to come forward to the altar. By this they would publicly affirm their commitment to the gospel. This was a physical expression of a spiritual reality, and as such it was powerful.

We do not do this so much anymore, and perhaps that is a shame. But just as preaching is feet first, so is the response of those who hear. God speaks and we are transformed. We rise up on our feet, and we go out into the world to which we have been called. We put our feet in motion, and only having done so might we use our tongues to speak the truth that we ourselves have heard. We preach, feet first, and as a result the people hear and are saved.

SUGGESTED READING

Adam, Peter. *Speaking God's Words: A Practical Theology of Expository Preaching.* Downers Grove, IL: InterVarsity, 1996.

Adams, Jay E. *Sense Appeal in the Sermons of Charles Haddon Spurgeon.* Grand Rapids: Baker, 1975.

Anderson, Kenton C. *Choosing to Preach: A Comprehensive Introduction to Sermon Options and Structures.* Grand Rapids: Zondervan, 2006.

Arthurs, Jeffrey. *Preaching with Variety: How to Recreate the Dynamics of Biblical Genres.* Grand Rapids: Kregel, 2007.

Bartow, Charles L. *God's Human Speech: A Practical Theology of Proclamation.* Grand Rapids: Eerdmans, 1997.

Bizzell, Patricia, and Bruce Herzberg. *The Rhetorical Tradition: Readings from Classical Times to the Present.* Boston: Bedford Books of St. Martin's, 1990.

Broadus, John Albert. *On the Preparation and Delivery of Sermons.* 4th ed. Revised by Vernon L. Stanfield. San Francisco: Harper & Row, 1979.

Buttrick, David. *Homiletic: Moves and Structures.* Philadelphia: Fortress, 1987.

Cahill, Dennis. *The Shape of Preaching: Theory and Practice in Sermon Design.* Grand Rapids: Baker Books, 2007.

Chapell, Bryan. *Christ-Centered Preaching: Redeeming the Expository Sermon.* Grand Rapids: Baker, 1994.

Craddock, Fred B. *As One without Authority.* 4th ed. St. Louis: Chalice, 2001.

Davis, Henry Grady. *Design for Preaching.* Philadelphia: Fortress, 1958.

Edwards, J. Kent. *Deep Preaching: Creating Sermons That Go beyond the Superficial.* Nashville: B&H, 2009.

Eslinger, Richard L. *A New Hearing: Living Options in Homiletic Method.* Nashville: Abingdon, 1987.

179

Fant, Clyde E. *Preaching for Today*. 2nd ed. San Francisco: Harper & Row, 1987.

Fulford, Robert. *The Triumph of Narrative: Storytelling in the Age of Mass Culture*. Toronto: Anansi, 1999.

Galli, Mark, and Craig Brian Larson. *Preaching That Connects: Using the Techniques of Journalists to Add Interest to Your Sermons*. Grand Rapids: Baker, 1994.

Goldsworthy, Graeme. *Preaching the Whole Bible as Christian Scripture: The Application of Biblical Theology to Expository Preaching*. Grand Rapids: Eerdmans, 2000.

Greidanus, Sidney. *The Modern Preacher and the Ancient Text: Interpreting and Preaching Biblical Literature*. Grand Rapids: Eerdmans, 1988.

Heisler, Greg. *Spirit-Led Preaching: The Holy Spirit's Role in Sermon Preparation and Delivery*. Nashville: B&H, 2007.

Johnson, Darrell W. *The Glory of Preaching: Participating in God's Transformation of the World*. Downers Grove, IL: IVP Academic, 2009.

Johnson, Patrick W. T. *The Mission of Preaching: Equipping the Community for Faithful Witness*. Downers Grove, IL: IVP Academic, 2015.

Kaiser, Walter, Jr. *Toward an Exegetical Theology: Biblical Exegesis for Preaching and Teaching*. Grand Rapids: Baker, 1981.

Keller, Timothy. *Preaching: Communicating Faith in an Age of Skepticism*. New York: Viking, 2015.

Koessler, John. *Folly, Grace, and Power: The Mysterious Act of Preaching*. Grand Rapids: Zondervan, 2011.

Kolb, David A. *Experiential Learning: Experience as the Source of Learning and Development*. Englewood Cliffs, NJ: Prentice-Hall, 1984.

Koller, Charles W. *Expository Preaching without Notes*. Grand Rapids: Baker, 1962.

Kuruvilla, Abraham. *Privilege the Text: A Theological Hermeneutic for Preaching*. Chicago: Moody, 2013.

Long, Thomas G. *The Witness of Preaching*. Louisville: Westminster John Knox, 1989.

Lowry, Eugene L. *Doing Time in the Pulpit: The Relationship between Narrative and Preaching*. Nashville: Abingdon, 1985.

———. *The Homiletic Plot: The Sermon as Narrative Art Form*. Atlanta: John Knox, 1980.

MacArthur, John, Jr. *Rediscovering Expository Preaching: Balancing the Science and Art of Biblical Exposition*. Dallas: Word, 1992.

Matthewson, Steven D. *The Art of Preaching Old Testament Narrative*. Grand Rapids: Baker Academic, 2002.

McClellan, Dave, and Karen McClellan. *Preaching by Ear: Speaking God's Truth from the Inside Out*. Wooster, OH: Weaver, 2014.

McDill, Wayne V. *The Moment of Truth: A Guide to Effective Sermon Delivery*. Nashville: B&H, 1999.

Ong, Walter J. *Orality and Literacy: The Technologizing of the Word*. New York: Routledge, 1982.

Quicke, Michael J. *360-Degree Preaching: Hearing, Speaking, and Living the Word*. Grand Rapids: Baker Books, 2011.

Reid, Robert Stephen. *The Four Voices of Preaching: The Connecting Purpose and Identity behind the Pulpit*. Grand Rapids: Brazos, 2006.

Richards, Larry. *Creative Bible Teaching*. Chicago: Moody, 1970.

Robinson, Haddon W. *Biblical Preaching: The Development and Delivery of Expository Sermons*. Grand Rapids: Baker, 1980.

Robinson, Haddon, and Craig Brian Larson, eds. *The Art and Craft of Biblical Preaching: A Comprehensive Resource for Today's Communicators*. Grand Rapids: Zondervan, 2005.

Smith, James K. A. *Desiring the Kingdom: Worship, Worldview, and Cultural Formation*. Grand Rapids: Baker Academic, 2009.

Smith, Robert, Jr. *Doctrine That Dances: Bringing Doctrinal Preaching and Teaching to Life*. Nashville: B&H, 2008.

Stewart, James. *Heralds of God*. 1946. Reprint, Vancouver: Regent College Publishing, 2001.

Stott, John R. W. *Between Two Worlds: The Art of Preaching in the Twentieth Century*. Grand Rapids: Eerdmans, 1982.

Walton, Benjamin H. *Preaching Old Testament Narratives*. Grand Rapids: Kregel, 2016.

Willard, Dallas. *The Divine Conspiracy: Rediscovering Our Hidden Life with God*. San Francisco: HarperSanFrancisco, 1998.

———. *The Spirit of the Disciplines: Understanding How God Changes Lives*. San Francisco: Harper & Row, 1988.

Wilson, Paul Scott. *The Practice of Preaching*. Nashville: Abingdon, 1995.

Wright, N. T. *Surprised by Hope: Rethinking Heaven, the Resurrection, and the Mission of the Church*. New York: HarperOne, 2008.

POSTSCRIPT

If you have found these materials helpful, I would encourage you to go to the integrative preaching website, found at www.preaching.org. There you will find additional materials helpful in learning and sharing these principles.

Along with posts and articles of relevance to the subject, the website features a series of visual presentations that you can use for yourself or use in teaching. There are also brief teaching videos that describe the contents of this model in a succinct form. I have included a fillable PDF that will be helpful as a tool for developing your sermon. Finally, you will find a selection of sample sermons that make use of all these tools. The web-based nature of this material will allow me to keep things current over time.

In addition, I would encourage you to follow me on Twitter @preachingdotorg. You can also find my personal feeds @kentoncanderson. Personal information can be found at www.kentoncanderson.com.

INDEX

abstraction, ladder of, 100
affection, 14
Amadeus (film), 95
anticipation, 73
appearance, 159–60
Apple (computer), 15
application, 80
apprehension, 96
Archimedes, 121, 131
Aristotle, 19
art, 112
assembly, 132, 133
attitude, 164
authority, 108

balance, 5
Bennett Dam, 153
brain science, 13
Browning, Robert, 25
Buttrick, David, 139

calling, 79
centripetal force, 10, 30
clothing. *See* appearance
cognitive, 14
coiling, 36, 40
coin (choice), 4
Collins, Jim, 6
complement, 61
compounds, 37, 85
confidence, 59
confusion, 62
context, 157

continuum (compromise), 5
convict, 66, 67, 96, 104
Craddock, Fred B., 121
cross, 6, 17, 30, 31

Davis, H. Grady, 112
deduction, 96
delivery, 155, 156
depth, 101
design, 112
dialogue, 158
discovery, 121, 122
distraction, 143
dress, 159–60

earth, 23
Edison, Thomas Alva, 87
Edwards, Jonathan, 81
elements, 35, 43
engage, 45, 46, 88, 111
event, 155, 156
examples, 128, 169
exegesis, 99
exposition, 126

Fasol, Al, 122
fear, 96, 164
finish, 141
fit, 135
"Five Whys," 92
flow, 141
Ford, Henry, 133
Francis of Assisi, 15
Fulford, Robert, 46

Galileo, 66, 74
gospel, 66, 68, 71
Grenz, Stanley, 72
Gretzky, Wayne, 73

Harrison, John, 166
head, 14
heart, 14
heaven, 24, 28
Hirsch, E. D., 113
Holy Spirit, xv, 73
horizontal axis, 2, 9, 11
Hubble Telescope, 110, 117

idea, 60
illustration, 50
images, 112
immediacy, 54
incarnation, 4
induction, 96
inertia, 34
inspire, 63, 76, 77, 104, 111
instruct, 56, 88, 96
integration, 3, 4, 8, 18
intention, 147
It Runs in the Family (film), 29

Kennedy, John F., 94
King, Martin Luther, Jr., 114
kingdom of God, 82
Kolb, David, 19, 30
Krakauer, Jon, 24

language, 141
Larson, Craig Brian, xii
latitude and longitude, 6
law, 28
leadership, xii, 156
Leonardo da Vinci, 76, 84
Lewis, C. S., 26
listening, xiii
logic, 62
Lovejoy, Grant, 160

Malone, Karl, 155
manuscript, of a sermon, 160
mastery, 145, 146
materials, 85, 127
memorization, 151
message, 121, 123, 147, 148
metaphor, 54, 142
method, 119
Minority Report (film), 29
mission, 76, 78, 81
model, 2
monologue, 158
motion, 34, 80
moviemakers, 54

objective, 26
objects, 162
Ong, Walter J., 150
orality, 150, 161
outcome, 145
ownership, 147

paralytic (Mark 2), 53, 54
pastor, 85, 90
Paul (apostle), 16
Philippians, 16

physical, 9, 12
pictures, 47, 48, 79, 110, 111, 114
points, 58, 70, 94, 95, 99
PowerPoint, 163
prayer, 70, 79, 102, 103, 107, 152
presence, 105
problems, 47, 49, 58, 85, 87, 88, 91
projection, 163
prophet, 113
propositions, 51
props, 162
pulpit, 162

reason, 96
reinforcement, 63
repetition, 141
Robinson, Haddon, 72, 100, 107

scientific method, 119
script, of a sermon, 160
Second Helvetic Confession, 77
sermon, 132, 149, 152
    manuscripting, 160–62
Sermon on the Mount, 27
sharing, 148
Shovell, Sir Cloudesley, 165
sin, 30
slide presentation, 163
space, for the Spirit, 73
speak, 149
spiritual axis, 9
spiritual formation, 38
Spurgeon, Charles, 114

Star Trek, 24, 45
story, 46
Stylites, Simeon, 11
subject, 61
subjective, 26
Sunukjian, Don, 91
Sweet, Leonard, xiii

Ten Commandments, 100
text, 126, 127
textopic, 124
theme, 56, 57, 59, 128
theologian, 94, 97
Thomas, Dylan, 26
time, 73, 137, 143, 148, 152, 166, 170
tone, 143, 157, 158
tools, 162
topic, 124
transposition, 52

U2 (band), 22
unction, 146
unity, 141

Vanauken, Sheldon, 20
vertical axis, 2, 9, 22, 26
video, 163
vision, 115
voice, 108

Willard, Dallas, 11, 28
word, 40, 64, 112, 166
worship, 18, 30
worshiper, 102, 105
Wright, N. T., 22, 28
Wright brothers (Wilber and Orville), 102, 108